MYSELF WHEN YOUNG

Growing Up in New York

1901–1925

D1457984

Also by Dr. Bishop

THE BIRTH OF A SPECIALTY:
   The Diary of
   An American Cardiologist   1926–1972

MYSELF
WHEN YOUNG

Growing Up in New York
1901–1925

LOUIS FAUGÈRES BISHOP, M.D.

The K. S. Giniger Company, Inc.
Publishers
New York

MYSELF WHEN YOUNG

Design by Harold Franklin

LIBRARY OF CONGRESS CATALOGUE CARD NUMBER: 85-071005

ISBN 0-934025-00-2

To our son

Louis Faugères Bishop III

CONTENTS

INTRODUCTION by *Norman Vincent Peale*   9

CHAPTER I   54 West 55th Street   13

    II Grandparents   18
        Mother / 25
        Father / 35

    III The Only Child   47

    IV St. Bernard's School   49
        Dancing School / 59

    V St. Paul's School   61
        Christmas Vacation / 64
        Games / 67
        Horatio Alger, Summer
          Vacations and War / 69
        Letters / 72
        Rosenbaum's / 73

    VI The Emmet Family   75
        My Friend Ingersoll / 79

    VII Yale: World War I and
        the Influenza Epidemic   84
        Sheffield Scientific
          School / 87
        Savin Rock / 90
        Sex Education / 91
        Riot / 93
        Fencing / 94
        Music and Theater / 97
        Traditions / 99
        Graduations / 100
        Epilogue / 101

CHAPTER

VIII European Trip   104
    London / 105
    Paris / 107
    Rome / 110
    Florence / 112
    Venice / 113
    More Paris / 113
    More London / 114
    Edinburgh and More
      of Scotland and
      England / 115
    London Again / 117

IX Medical School   118

X Celebrities   138
    Clubs / 143
    Games I Have Played / 147

XI Religion   154

XII Marriage   156

XIII Epilogue   158

INTRODUCTION

DR. LOUIS FAUGÈRES BISHOP, the author of this delightful auto-biographical volume, *Myself When Young*, has been my personal physician and friend for close to fifty years. And he is uniquely great in both capacities.

Some years ago, in London, I began to feel unwell and had a bad time with dizziness and the like. After a concert in Royal Albert Hall, it got worse and we had enormous difficulty getting a taxi to the hotel. "If I can get home to see Louis Bishop," I told my wife, Ruth, "then everything will be all right."

When, finally, I did get back home to his office on East 60th Street, he went over me in his calm, very thorough way and authoritatively declared, "You're all right! Just pushing yourself too hard, as usual. Ease up." All at once I felt perfectly well. Such is my supreme confidence in this great physician.

Then, with my usual drive, I jumped up to pursue my customary fast pace. Louis looked over his glasses, "I said, 'ease up' and we will keep you going strong for years to come."

He is one of those great doctors just to be with whom seems to make you well. At least he has been doing that with me for half a century. To a pronounced degree, he has the healing touch.

Dr. Bishop ranks high in his profession. He was one of the founders of the New York Cardiological Society and later its president. When the American College of Cardiology emerged from the New York society, he was made a trustee. Later, in 1960–61, he was the distinguished president of the American College of Cardiology. The college has played a major role in the continuing education of physicians in cardiovascular disease. Not long ago the American College of Cardiology established a lectureship in his name, further honoring Dr. Bishop for his outstanding achievements in this field.

The senior Dr. Louis Faugères Bishop, Louis' father, whom I knew well, was considered the first heart specialist in the United States and was a pioneer on the use of the electrocardiograph. Incidentally, during his presidency of this great national medical organization, he invited me to talk at the annual convention held in New York. When I demurred on the grounds of not being a medical man, he turned off my protestations, declaring that doctors needed "positive thinking" the same as anyone.

We have read innumerable stories of poor boys who made good. This is the story of a rich boy who made good. It's a kind of reverse Horatio Alger narrative. Not an up-from-the-bottom, but rather an on up from the top story. And it is just as interesting as any of the usual success books.

As a longtime New Yorker, I find Dr. Bishop's book fascinating as a graphic and nostalgic picture of the way it was in New York in the first twenty-five years of this century. And because the great city is a romantic place in the minds of all Americans, this well-written story of life in the metropolis in those days will be of great interest to every reader.

Louis Bishop is rare good company, a delightful companion to be with. He is a capital raconteur and he writes just as he talks. Growing up in New York in a socially prominent family, Dr. Bishop mirrors a life style that has intrigued many. But it is an inspiring American story as well, for the boy reared in this elite atmosphere became one of the great physicians of his time, giving loving service to all people. In this book, you will meet a lovable personality; his fascinating story will give you much pleasure.

NORMAN VINCENT PEALE

MYSELF WHEN YOUNG

Growing Up in New York

1901–1925

Chapter I

54 West 55th Street

IN 1901, NEW YORK'S 55TH STREET, between Fifth and Sixth Avenues, was made up primarily of houses with brownstone fronts. These brownstone houses, so-called because they had been built of easily available reddish brown sandstone or were faced with that material, were not lookalikes, for each had its own style of entrance and individual facade and they were of varying sizes.

Our house was a simple one, with a stoop or brownstone steps leading up to the entrance. There was also a basement entrance for delivery men where, if you pulled a wrought iron knob, a bell jangled inside. The two front windows were protected against burglars by iron grilles on the exterior. There was a sitting room for the servants in front and, in the back, was the kitchen, which overlooked the backyard where laundry was hung to dry. The backyard also had other uses as far as I was concerned—it was possible to play ball in it. At an early age, I was learning to high jump and this was a place where I could practice. I do not believe I was allowed to play in the street—I do not remember doing so.

Across from us on 55th Street was Browning School, an important school for young boys, which exists to this day. Its counterpart was Spence School for young girls, named for its famous schoolmistress. Miss Spence, is, of course, still known not only in New York, but all over the world. At that time, more emphasis was put on the social graces, but I think schools today, do put more emphasis on education.

On the north side, at Fifth Avenue, was the Fifth Avenue Presbyterian Church and, in 1904, on the south corner, the Gotham Hotel was opened. It was very elegant; I remember being taken there for haircuts. I don't remember eating there because, at that time, people rarely ate out, unless they were going to the theatre.

As an infant, I would be taken in a baby carriage to Central Park by my nurse, Mary Smith. She was Irish, born in the

County Cavan. The Irish nurses who took care of the children of well-to-do families in New York could be compared to the nannies of the affluent upper class English families. These Irish nannies had a special place in the household. They also had a definite "aristocracy" of their own and took their charges to

Age Two.

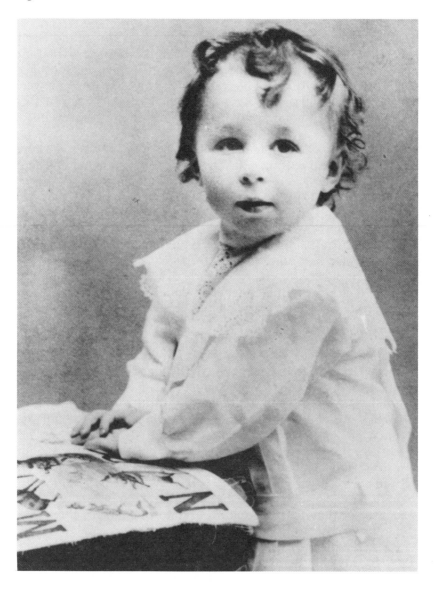

special areas in the park, where children would associate with others of the same social background.

Mary Smith stayed with the family until I went to boarding school and then she returned to Ireland. As did all boys who had Irish nurses, I became very attached to Mary Smith. She did not replace my mother, as was the case in some families, but I was upset to see her go.

Our house consisted of four floors. The first floor was used by my father as his office and we lived above. Rarely now do physicians have their offices in their homes in New York. My father's office had a waiting room and a large office in the rear, which combined a consulting room and examining room. The patient undressed behind a screen and then placed himself or herself on the examining table. In those early days, my father was a general practitioner and, besides medicine, he did a certain amount of minor surgery as well as office gynecology.

On the second floor, there was a living room in front and, in the rear, a dining room. Both rooms were ornate, furnished with crystal chandeliers, French gilt and Empire furniture, some of which remains in the family to this day. We had a lovely bannister between the second floor and the first. I would often slide down it instead of descending the stairs, sometimes landing with a loud thud. My mother would admonish me that I must be quiet, as my father had a patient in his first floor office. Later, when I became a doctor myself, I understood.

My mother loved to entertain and gave many parties. Nearly always these were formal dinner parties. The men wore full dress, arriving with top hats and big overcoats; sometimes they wore capes. The ladies wore elegant long gowns.

Warm dishes, roasts, vegetables could be pulled up from the kitchen on the ground floor to the dining room by means of a dumbwaiter, a small, rope-drawn, hand-operated elevator. I remember that, during one of my mother's dinner parties, the conveyor broke and all her best dishes fell to the basement. I was not present, of course, but I was told how well she had weathered this, acting the perfect hostess, as though nothing had happened.

My mother had a full-time cook and several maids to serve. After dinner, as was the custom, the men were left alone to their brandy and cigars; later joining the ladies in the living room to play cards. A simple form of bridge was played, not the "Chicago" or rubber bridge played today.

There were, it seemed to me, always plenty of servants. I never knew my mother to do any household work herself. It wasn't that she couldn't, but it was not the social custom of the day for the lady of the house to do this. We had a waitress who waited on table and I think she answered the doorbell. A chambermaid did the cleaning of the house. Another handled the laundry. They were all typical Irish old maids.

My mother had a large number of clocks. In fact, she had so many that it was necessary to have a clock winder come in at periodic intervals. Someone else came in to clean the silver. The bookcases were rarely opened and contained the usual beautifully bound classic sets. They were kept in good condition.

On the third floor, with a somewhat shorter staircase, were the large bedrooms—mine was in back and my mother and father were in front. A bathroom adjoined my room and, being an only child, I lived rather luxuriously and did not have to share this with brothers and sisters. Over the tub was a picture of the Matterhorn. Years later, when I saw this mountain in Switzerland, I thought to myself, "It looks just like the picture."

On the fourth floor, were the servants' quarters. There were four rooms. The front room was occupied by my Uncle Ben, who lived with us and was very good to me while I was growing up.

Uncle Ben was a rare character. He had lived in the West and he was always telling me about his life with the cowboys and the Indians. I was fascinated. I am not sure whether all of it was true, but it did intrigue a little boy. He had been married, but I never knew what had become of his wife.

He was supposed to stay only a short time, but Uncle Ben ended up remaining for a long time. He did many things for me, including, knowing that I liked to jump, building a high jump for me and adjusting the heights. It was the sort of thing used in athletic contests. It was in my room; I worked at it and won a few high jump contests in school.

Uncle Ben liked the movies and would take me to a movie from time to time. He had no children himself, and he took an interest in me and was a real companion.

He was very good with his hands and could fix things that went wrong with the house. My father was also away a good deal and Uncle Ben, in a protective way, acted as the man of the house when my father was out.

He later worked for my father in his office, but retired after he inherited some money. He also remarried late in life.

In retrospect, I think that the home in which I grew up was typical of the homes of the New York upper middle class.

I recently walked through 55th Street. The brownstone front,

No. 54, where I was born, is still there, but the front stoop has been removed, as in nearly all the buildings on the street. There was a delicatessen on the street floor and a beauty parlor on the "parlor" floor. The Gotham Hotel was being renovated to become the Nova Park-Gotham. But the Fifth Avenue Presbyterian Church is still there.

Spence and Browning Schools are long gone to other areas. As I came to Sixth Avenue, I wondered how many people remembered the elevated train that ran up to 59th Street. Luxurious apartment buildings now line the west side of the street to the north, now called the Avenue of the Americas, where originally there had been little shops and my mother had done her marketing. I particularly remember a candy store, with the unusual name of "Hoops," where we found candy and ice cream sodas. There was also a restaurant there called The Alps, recently recalled to me by a friend. We both remembered wallpaper depicting scenes of Switzerland.

The brownstone fronts, as we knew them, are no more. But they had strength and beauty.

Chapter II

Grandparents

I NEVER SAW MY PATERNAL GRANDPARENTS, but my father told me a lot about them. My paternal grandfather, James Bishop, was a very colorful character and had several varied careers. First, he was in business and eventually ended his career in the New Jersey legislature, where he apparently sided with the labor movement of that period.

After his business suffered reverses in which he lost a fortune, he was returning to America from Europe, when he was shipwrecked. He managed to survive by climbing on a plank and was rescued. The story of the wreck is well-documented in the diary which he kept:

Saturday, November 15, 1873
Left New York by Steam Ship Ville du Havre, Captain Surmont, at 2:30 p.m. Weather pleasant with aboard 80 cabin passengers. Sea very smooth so that all sat down to a good dinner at 4:30 p.m.

Sunday, November 16, 1873
After a very quiet night all the passengers seemed bright and cheerful this morning, most of them appearing on deck. There was no service this morning but at half past seven in the evening the service of the Episcopal Church was read in the salon. Made 200 miles to 12 o'clock.

Monday, November 17, 1873
This morning the wind came up from the south east bringing with it a rolling sea which made the greater part of the women and children sick—very few appearing at meals. Made 235 miles to 12 o'clock.

Tuesday, November 18, 1873
The south east storm still continues and the sea increasing in high waves. There are a large number of children on board and almost all of them are sick. Toward night

the wind increased to a gale and the ship rolled heavily so that passengers were thrown from one side of the cabin to the other. Made 245 miles.

Wednesday, November 19, 1873

After a very rough night the wind subsided and changed more to the south, enabling the ship to carry some sail which steadied her considerably. The sun shone out during the morning but a fog set in about noon requiring the use of a fog whistle constantly. Made 250 miles to 12, M.

Thursday, November 20, 1873

The morning still very foggy, the fog whistle having been blown nearly all night. The stateroom leaked so badly that my bed being wet I did not undress last night but lay down on the lounge getting what sleep I could. The whole day dull. Made 270 miles to 12, M.

Friday, November 21, 1873

Weather still foggy with wind south blowing moderately—sea smooth and all passengers enjoying themselves.

(Left) *Portrait of James Bishop believed to have been painted about 1865.* **(Right)** *Paternal grandmother, Mary Faugères Bishop, painted at the same time.*

A large number of children on board and all full of spirit in the cabin. The ship having lost one flange the propeller retards her progress and will prolong the voyage. 280 miles to 12, M.

Saturday, November 22, 1873

Went to bed about 11:00 o'clock Friday night, weather clear, wind moderate from the south, forward and main sails drawing well. Having been anxious for two or three nights on account of the thick fog so that I did not undress, I prepared myself fully for bed and soon slept soundly. About two o'clock in the morning Saturday was awakened by a loud noise and the jar of a sudden crash. I immediately jumped from my berth and on opening my door saw Mr. Taylor in the passageway, who immediately called out "Bishop, something awful has happened." I then went into the passage and heard a few yards toward the stern screams and cries of persons in great distress. I then returned to my room and hastily put on a part of my clothing and with Mr. Taylor went on deck by the stairway forward, the other end of the passage being blocked up by the broken litter of the cabin which had been crushed in.

When on deck at once the fact was realized that the ship must go down. Proceeded aft and saw the starboard boat, where the ship was struck, was stove in and lay on deck. The two whale boats near the stern were being lowered by the ships crew and men were at work at the two large boats near the midships. The large boat on the port side was apparently in the water when the mainmast fell with a crash on that side of the ship, burying the boat and persons in it under its ruin. The mizzen mast immediately followed and the whole of the deck toward the stern was covered with ruin and many persons were either killed or greatly injured. I then went to the starboard boat near the Captain's room and found a great number of men working on it, but for some cause the iron davits did not work and the boat could not be gotten over the side of the ship.

During this time the passengers were moving about in the quiet of despair. No screams nor lamentations were heard, but many an audible prayer was uttered. My friend, Mr. Taylor kept near me most of the time and we soon concluded we must prepare to count much to the mercy of God on the sea, as the ship was settling rapidly. I went down the forecastle and brought out two planks found under the carpenter's bench and gave one to Mr. Taylor as we could not find a life preserver.

Just as the waves began to wash over the deck Mr. Taylor and myself got outside the ship's rail and sprung into the sea with our planks, he proceeding me only a few seconds. This we did fearing to be drawn down into the vortex of the sinking ship. I had succeeded in getting about 30 yards from the ship when she made a plunge forward and settled immediately out of sight leaving a mass of wrecked matter with hundreds of human beings struggling and screaming in the agonies of despair and death. I was only partially drawn back by the succeeding wave caused by the sinking hulk, and then with the support of the plank attempted to swim toward the vessel which had done us the injury, apparently not more than ½ mile distant.

I was enabled to make some progress when I soon encountered a large piece of the wrecked ship upon which only one man was clinging. To this I immediately attached my own plank and remained until one of the boats of the French ship came near enough to be hailed and we were both taken on board. The person clinging with me proved to be Captain Surmont of the Ville du Havre.

After picking up as many as the boat could safely carry we were taken on board the ship Loch Earn, Captain Robinson, the vessel which had been in collision with us. It was now about ½ past 3 a.m. and my watch was stopped at ½ past two. The Ville du Havre could not have been above water more than 15 or 20 minutes at the longest, from the moment of collision.

The Ville du Havre sank at 47° N latitude and 38° W longitude, in mid-Atlantic, one of the deepest parts of the Atlantic Ocean.

The ship Loch Earn having its bowsprit completely carried away and a large number of her iron plates crushed inward, leaving an opening in her bow, reaching nearly to her water line, tho only in ballast, it was disposed unsafe for the wrecked persons to remain on board, consequently a signal was raised for a ship which appeared in sight quite early and she immediately stood by for us and by 12 o'clock all were safely placed on board the American ship Tremontain, Captain Urquhart, loaded with grain and bound for Bristol, England.

No kinder treatment could possibly be received from human hands than Captain Urquhart tendered to us. All were, of course, scantily clad, and especially to the ladies were his rooms given, clothing left by his wife who had accompanied him on the previous voyage promptly furnished, and every possible comfort administered. Never, never can any of us forget the warm sympathy and kindness of the Captain and officers of the Tremontain.

Finally:
Reached Cardiff (England) and came to anchor 5 miles below at 10 o'clock during the evening, December 1, 1873.

In the diary is a list of the total number of people on board the Ville du Havre and those saved:

Officers and Crew	172
1st Class	89
2nd Class	19
3rd Class	27
Stowaways	6
	313
Saved	87
Lost	226

Of the 87 saved, the record specifies:

Crew	53
Officers	6
Passengers	27
Stowaways	1
Total saved	87

There is evidence that James Bishop was rich at one time, as his fine house may still be seen in New Brunswick and is now part of Rutgers University. There is a street there called Bishop Place. It interested me that the Bishop family is a part of New Jersey history.

My paternal grandmother had a social background in New York. My father preserved all her letters, and it was apparent that she kept in close contact with all her children. She would be considered a classic "Jewish mother" for she followed every

Paternal grandfather, James Bishop's house, New Brunswick, New Jersey, now part of the Rutgers campus.

detail of her childrens' lives. From the pictures I have seen of her, she was the most attractive of my relatives of that time. Her name was Mary Faugères, a name I eventually inherited.

My mother's father was totally different from my Bishop grandfather. He had had a remarkable career. Born Siegfried Gruner in Germany, he came here at an early age and went into the cotton business. He was successful financially and socially and ended his career as president of the Cotton Exchange, where his picture still hangs. He died suddenly, aged fifty, at the St. Regis Hotel, as he was tying his shoelaces.

I did not know him, but I did know my maternal grandmother and, in many ways, she, too, was most unusual. I called her Mama Gruner; in later life she became "the Countess" to many people, when she married a French count. I do not remember ever seeing him but, as you might imagine, he was not very popular in the family.

The story about the count's death in Paris always interested me. Apparently, he liked to gamble and, with my grandmother's money, he had ample opportunity. In all events, when he was found to have a deck of cards that contained five aces, in-

Maternal grandparents, Annie and Siegfried Gruner.

stead of the usual four, he was shot and that was the last heard about him. I believe that, in Paris at that time, it was permissible to shoot anyone caught cheating at cards.

There were other interesting points about the countess. In later life, I would say in her late 60's, she rode to hounds. As I understand it, foxhunting calls for expert horsemanship and also a good deal of nerve. She also had that indefinable quality called charm. The dictionary has one definition of charm as follows: "a trait that fascinates, allures, or delights." She passed this on to her son, Harry, and to some extent, to my mother.

It was unfair, but her main interest was her son and he received most of her wordly goods. My mother told the story of coming home; her mother calling out, "Is that you, dear?"; and my mother answering, "No, mother, it's only me."

My uncle Harry was a good son to the countess and he never

missed a day seeing her when she finally came to live in New York. She preferred Europe, particularly the Riviera and for many years had an apartment in Nice.

Before I married, my future wife visited her in Europe and she insisted on getting my fiancée a gigolo to take her dancing.

MOTHER

There is little one can add to the mother-son relationship that has not been said before. It can be a difficult relationship when one is an only son, as well as an only child, as in my case. My relationship with my mother, however, was a happy one.

My mother was often asked by her friends why she had had only one child. Her reply was: "Have you read Aesop's *Fa-*

Four generations. Mother, Grandmother Gruner, Great-grandmother Dater.

bles? The reason I ask is to remind you of the story about the lioness who was questioned by the monkey why she had only one offspring. Her answer was, 'I don't have to worry, because he is a Lion!' ''

I was brought up during the period when a mother, if financially able, entrusted her children to a nurse (in my case the Irish Mary Smith.) My mother spent little time with me and our real relationship only began when I was old enough to go out with her. I have no recollection of her ever wheeling me in a baby carriage or taking me to the park. This was left entirely to Mary.

Mary Smith was a typical example of the Irish nanny who existed in the New York in which I was growing up. She did everything for me. I vaguely remember that, when I went into long pants, my mother then took part in selecting my clothes, but not before.

Mary took me to the 59th Street entrance of Central Park, opposite the Plaza Hotel, where we would meet other children and their Irish nannies. The young women would talk and visit, while the children played. Later, Mary took me to school and called for me, until finally I rebelled and demanded to go alone.

The Irish nanny's place in the household was a little higher than that of the other servants. She had no other duties than my care. As you might expect, Mary was a Catholic and, because of that, I absorbed a certain amount of Catholicism, which didn't do me any harm.

Finally, I was to go to boarding school, and Mary's job was done. She went back to Ireland, I believe to Country Cavan. The influence of an Irish nanny cannot be understated. They were good people.

A few years ago, I heard my mother described as a "German Mother," one who hovers over and overindulges her children. I am sure I was overindulged. On the other hand, she was anxious for me to experience discipline early in life, and had, therefore, decided to send me to an English school.

As an only child, I did spend more time with her when I was growing up, than if I had had other brothers or sisters. My mother, without realizing it, transmitted many of her own interests to me. As in the case of my father, I absorbed a good deal of her thinking.

My mother's German background was always apparent to me. She would often refer to her German cousins and she described a wedding she had attended as a young girl, where she had met a young German officer with whom she had had a flirtation. She spoke German to her German friends and often used German phrases, which expressed her thought better than English. I was

(Left) *Grandmother Gruner and daughter, Charlotte, c. 1870's.*
(Right) *The 'Merry Villagers'. Mother and a friend.*

always aware that there was a second language in the house. Having a grandfather named Siegfried Gruner, how could it be otherwise! I later heard, but could not verify, that Wagner died the year her father was born and most boys born that year in Germany were named Siegfried.

My mother had married my father, the "poor doctor," against her family's wishes and his relationship with his new in-laws was unpleasant. It was not until much later, when my father had become a world figure in medicine, that her family accepted him.

I think my mother was much responsible for his success, for she was very gay and loved parties; she created a happy environment for him. My father was a thoughtful, serious man and, in his own way, he enjoyed the aura of gaiety that surrounded her. She once told me that she had never gotten my father a patient, but she added, "I never lost one for him, either." The house was always filled with her friends, whom my father called "the Merry Villagers."

In her own way, my mother influenced me differently than my father. I sensed that he hoped I would follow in his footsteps and become a doctor. My mother would question me about this. As the wife of a doctor, she was aware of the complete dedication necessary to follow a medical career, and I think she wished a less demanding life for me. She might have preferred me to study finance and business with a view to the brokerage business, the world in which she had grown up. She liked the idea of gambling and the big money to be made at that time "on the street." Her brother, Harry, was a broker, and his fortunes varied from day to day. My mother told me that when my grandfather would come home after a day on the Exchange, she could tell how the market had closed that day by how he slammed the front door.

In our family, on my father's side, was a rich relative, an aged bachelor, president of a rubber company. My mother, in her wisdom, officially made him my godfather. I was told that whenever he came to the house, I was to call him "Godfather," and be on my good behavior. He was a nice old boy, with a speech impediment, so I had difficulty understanding what he said. His main interest, outside of his business, was yacht racing, which brought him close to my father, who also loved boats. My godfather owned one of the best of the American racing yachts, the *Katrina*. I was too young at the time, but my father often sailed with him.

My mother's interest in our rich relative paid off, as far as I was concerned, for every Christmas I would be formally called to his office, where I would be given a present in the form of bonds, which I would bring home to the family to keep for me. Later in life, afraid that I would blow this capital, I put it into a irrevocable trust for the benefit of my family.

My godfather sometimes presented a problem because, at my mother's Christmas parties, he would proceed to get "fractured," and have to be taken home. This was often difficult on the usually snowy Christmas Eves when all means of transportation disappeared. He would take with him the beautifully wrapped present, some unusual gift my mother had sought out.

Sadly, when he died, we found in his closet all the Christmas presents, still wrapped and never opened. It turned out that he left a part of his fortune to my father, whom he greatly admired, and this enabled my father to retire after his brilliant career. Other family members had tried to cultivate our rich relative, but my mother had staved off the competition.

There was a thoughtful side to my mother. Although she was in no sense a bibliophile, she had some favorite authors, one being Charles Dickens. She would often refer to one of his

Godfather James Bishop Ford, president of the United States Rubber Company.

characters. Later, when I traveled, I would bring her a porcelain figure of a Dickens character, and eventually she had a fine collection.

She also had a great love of poetry, which she tried to impart to me. When she died, I found a book she had which was titled, *Reveries of a Maid*. In it she had copied various quotations and poems that she particularly liked. Most of what was in the book, she had read as a student at Brearly School. For the most part the poems are romantic and quite beautiful, but neither the poems nor the poets are familiar to us today. One poem was entitled "Indian Summer," and particularly interests me as I am writing this on an Indian summer day:

Indian Summer

Yes the Indian summer lingers still
The hazes loiter on the hill
The year a spendthrift growing old
Is scattering his lavish gold
For a last pleasure.
The robins flock but do not go
We share the wood with footsteps slow
In sober leisure
Or sit beneath the chestnut tree
Our hands in silent company.
Not yet, dear friend, we part, not yet.
Full soon the last warm sun will set
The crickets cease to stir the grass
The gold and amber fade away.
The scarlet from the landscape pass
And all the sky be sodden gray
Too soon alas the frost must fall
And blight the astors on the hill
The golden rod the gentians all
And we must feel this parting chill
But oh not yet, not yet we part
The summer strains us to the heart
The world is all a golden smile
And we may love a little while
The summer dies and hearts forget
And we must part, not yet, not yet.

(Author unknown to me)

My mother loved the theatre, and would often take me alone
to a matinee. Another poem in her book is called, ''The End of
the Play,'' its author unknown:

The play is done, the curtain drops
Slow falling to the prompters bill.
A moment yet the actor stops
And looks around to say farewell.
It is an irksome work and task
And when he's laughed and said his say,
He shows as he removes the mask
A face that's anything but gay.

Mother.

From her early days, she had a great love of Christmas, and there appears also a poem called, "Let Us Keep Christmas" by Grace Noll Crowell:

Whatever else be lost among the years,
Let us keep Christmas still a shining thing.
Whatever doubts assail us or what fears,
Let us hold close remembering
Its poignant meaning for the years of men.
Let us back our faith again.

Wealth may have taken wings, yet still there are
Clear window panes to glow with candlelight.
There are boughs for garlands and a tinsel star
To top some little fir tree's lifted height.
There is no heart too heavy or too sad
But some small gift of love can make it glad.

And there are home sweet rooms where laughter rings
And we sing the carols as of old.
Above the Eastern hills a white star swings.
There is an ancient story to be told.
There are kind words and cheering words to say.
Let us be happy on the Christ Child's Day.

This piece about Christmas was reflected in all her Christmas parties. The star was always on top of the tree. There was a small gift for everyone and the old carols were always played and sung. Her family and friends were happy on the "Christ Child's Day."

My mother had her own ideas about money. Although she had not had any formal training regarding finance, she had her own thoughts about handling it. She had been brought up in a home where money was never a problem, whereas my father had had to be very careful about money. Someone once asked her if she knew anything about arithmetic, and her answer was that although she could not add, she knew how to subtract.

Whatever money my father gave her, which was in addition to her income from a trust, she would put some of it into stocks. There was only one in which she had faith and that was AT&T, which in itself showed some financial judgment.

She never thought my father tipped enough and she would frequently add to whatever he gave for service. This never bothered him. In fact, anything she did was all right with him.

As far as I was concerned, she was very generous and, when

I needed extra money, she gave it to me. This is, perhaps, not the way to train a boy in the value of money, but it didn't seem to bother her. Several times, a fairly large amount of money would be involved. Once, during my college days, I went to Montreal and ended up at a racetrack called Blue Bonnets. There I proceeded to lose all I had with me. I was alone, with no way of getting back. I did not want to call my father, because gambling was one pastime of which he did not approve. I called my mother, who wired the money, with no lecture.

I cannot remember any time of trouble when she did not help. When she was very old and I had just returned from war, I needed capital to start over again. She lent me some securities my father had left her, against which I could borrow. I remember what she said when she did this, "Well, my son, I guess we will have to milk the cow." It seemed very appropriate.

She had no knowledge of nor any interest in the Internal Revenue Service. When I told her she would have to pay taxes on some stock she had in her box, she said, "How does the government know it's there?"

In spite of her generosity, she was careful. She gambled at bridge for modest stakes. She also had a bookmaker. I suspect it was her grocer who handled her two dollar bets on the horses and occasionally she would bet on a Yale game when I told her I thought we had a good chance.

She was always concerned about my financial future and felt that I ought to have capital separate from what I earned. Enjoying a little gambling herself, I think she feared I might take to it, too.

My mother's last years give insight into her character. It is said that when one gets old, traits become more evident. My mother developed Parkinson's disease and eventually became a total invalid. In most cases, this disease allows the brain to remain clear. In spite of the fact that she became more and more helpless, she never complained. She remained the hostess, and would be dressed and ready to greet her guests, mostly family now, who would come to see her. "Will you have a cocktail?" she would ask, regardless of the time of day, and she kept a supply of bottled cocktails, easily made, so guests could help themselves.

She remained interested in family problems, but her main interest was in me and what she could do for me. When I would tell her about the office and medical meetings I had attended or taken part in, her remark was always the same, "Your father would have been proud of you."

She kept up with current events by radio and television, which

Father.

at that time was just coming into the home.

My own family were very good to her, and I managed to see her every day. She made few jaunts from her apartment, but her nurse did take her, in a wheelchair and with some difficulty, to the movie, "Gigi," which takes place in the era she knew so well. She loved the music, the gowns, the color and, when it ended, she refused to go and insisted on sitting through it again.

My mother finally reached the point where she was bedridden. Her nurse over the many years wanted to go home to Ireland to live and so I decided to move her to a hospital for chronic care. I have always thought it a mistake to move an elderly person from their home and it may well be true, because my mother died a few days later. She was ninety years old.

In later life, someone asked me about my relationship with my mother. My answer was that I was very fond of her, because she was the only one I ever knew who thought I was perfect.

FATHER

The father-son relationship can be even more complex than the mother-son relationship. The father, particularly if he is successful in business or in a profession, wants his son to follow in his footsteps. This is not always possible, as we all know. The son may not live up to the expectations of his father, which can cause real conflict. If he is an only son, the expectations for what he will accomplish are even greater.

All of this applied to my relationship with my father, but I feel that my father had a good influence on my future life. I was very fond of my mother, and I do think my conversations with my father regarding the mother-son relationship made me more aware that she might someday need me. I was too young at the time to appreciate my father's intellect and what a fine mind he had. But he did impart many things that have remained important to me.

Although I did not know it when I was young, I was what we now call a "celebrity kid." My father's importance in the world came into focus during my teen years, when we went to the European spa, Bad Nauheim, and I realized that many people depended on him. Later, when I started medical school, I realized that my father was one of the best-known physicians in New York, perhaps in the country, or indeed in the world, as he was considered the first heart specialist in the United States.

The story of my father as heart specialist really begins with his realization of the importance of a specialist. It all started on the coast of Maine, where my family took me in the summer. The name of the place was York Harbor. At that time, 1908, it was a well known summer resort. I believe it still is but I have never been there since. My father did what was then called general practice at York Harbor—meaning he took care of practically everything except major surgery. It would be unlikely that there would be any other type of doctor in such a place.

At all events, so I heard, a baby with a heart murmur came under his care. My father told the family it had, as far as he was concerned, no significance and, in all probability, the infant would outgrow it. He charged his usual fee for a visit to the office (located in the house that we rented), which was about five dollars. The family, upon hearing about the murmur in their infant child, went into an immediate panic and wanted a consultation. A consultant was called from Boston. There were no cardiologists or heart specialists in those days, but the consultants were supposed to have a special knowledge about any part of the body. The consultant arrived, told the family that my father was correct, that it was an innocent murmur, and departed for Boston. I don't know what his fee was, but it was not five dollars, I am sure. My mother told me the following day that

With Mother and Father in Atlantic City, about 1906.

Bad Nauheim, c. 1910.

my father decided to give up general practice and become a consultant with a special knowledge.

The special knowledge he acquired eventually was about the heart. It took a long time for the general consultants to recognize that anyone could have a greater knowledge of this particular organ than they did. As a result, anyone who even claimed this was vigorously opposed.

But, first, my father had to acquire this special knowledge. At the time, there seemed to be a greater knowledge of the heart in Europe than in America, and the best known heart center in the world was in Bad Nauheim, Germany. So that is where he went to study, with German heart specialists, to learn their methods and treatments and bring them back to America.

I was very young at the time and only interested in playing golf and tennis, but I do have a clear recollection of how hard he worked, as my mother and I rarely saw him in the day time. The only thing I do remember is while we were there, in 1914, war broke out and we had to get out in a hurry.

My father did bring back to America a knowledge of the heart that very few men had and it wasn't very long before he became recognized as a heart specialist. This was clearly evident, because when doctors got a heart condition, they would go to him. As a result, a large number of his patients were other physicians.

He continued to develop his knowledge by going to England where the heart specialist was already recognized and the great Sir James Mackenzie was thought of by the British as the first to specialize in the study of heart disease. My father and Mackenzie became great friends. In my office, I have a framed letter from him to my father, telling him to come back to see him.

Sir Thomas Lewis was developing the study of electrocardiography and my father had brought one of the first machines to America. It took a long time before it was thought to be of any practical value because very few understood it.

These things gave my father the claim of being the first or at very least among the first of the American heart specialists.

I have few recollections as a very young child of my father, except that he was there. When I got older, he would find opportunities to spend time with me. Although he had little interest in tennis or golf, and little skill in these sports, he played with me. In return, although I had no interest in sailing, which he very much enjoyed, I would sail with him.

Except for his interest in sports as a form of exercise, he had little interest in profesional or amateur sports. At that time we did not have television, which I think fosters one's interest in sports. He was very loyal to Rutgers as far as football was concerned, and he did tell me that he helped Paul Robeson, who went on to become a national figure, at Rutgers. Eventually, my father became a trustee of Rutgers.

The shipping interests of my grandfather and great-grandfather had strongly influenced my father. He often spoke of the time in 1854 that his father's clipper ship had made the trip from New York around Cape Horn to San Francisco in the record time of 105 days, a feat in those days.

My father's sailboat was a small one that he kept at the Seawanhaka Yacht Club. We took part in races on Saturday afternoons and it interested me that my father never seemed to care whether we won or lost. As a result, we were usually last, except on one occasion when we unexpectedly won. This happened because he took a different course than the rest of the fleet and found an unexpected wind which put us in front by a wide margin. This was our only triumph.

I was reminded of my father recently when I heard my son-in-law, presiding at a meeting of new members of a society, use the expression "welcome aboard." My father was fond of using certain sea expressions handed down for generations by those who loved ships and sailing. We had to keep everything "shipshape." We had always to have "an anchor to windward." I am not sure what that means, but probably you ought to have something to fall back on, if you fail at something—some insurance in case things don't go right.

Another expression he used was, "Always keep your end up," which meant do your share. Those who "don't keep their end up," soon are shunned. If someone buys you a drink, you return it at some time; you don't just forget it. My father was very careful about this. There was never any question of "sponging." Later on in life I saw instances of this, and remembered my father's strong feelings about it. And he would say, when I would fail to do something, that "there are no alibis." This has stuck with me, that there are no reasons for not doing what one is supposed to do.

I often think of a bit of advice he gave me regarding dress. He often said to me, "If you have anything important to do, dress up for the occasion"—show by your dress that it is important. I notice today around New York all sorts of costumes. Of course, in those days, dressing was more formal than even our well-dressed people do today. This idea has remained with me and, even today, I am conscious of "dressing up," when I have a special appointment or a special lunch.

He also sent me to the good stores. Amory, in Scott Fitzgerald's *This Side of Paradise*, is told by his mother, "You must go to Brooks and get some really nice suits." This is not unlike the advice from my father. Brooks was then, and still is, a good store for young men.

When I got older, my father sent me to his tailor to have clothes made. He himself always looked well, never sloppy, shoes always polished, clean shirt. From this early exposure, I went on to appreciate the London tailors.

I have carried his advice to me on these and other subjects throughout my life and, although they were verbal, they were not unlike the advice given by Lord Chesterfield to his son, in his classic letters.

Spending time with my father, I learned much about his philosophy and religion. I had been to St. Paul's School and so had he; we had been brought up as rather strict Episcopalians in the tradition of the school. Before St. Paul's, he had been brought up in the Methodist Church. My father believed in all faiths. He believed that what was important was to follow a faith, whatever it might be, and that one should respect the beliefs of others. Later on, he wrote several papers on the relationship between medicine and religion. He had a great friend, Dr. Wade, with a congregation down in Greenwich Village, whom he visited often, and I recall my father once speaking from Dr. Wade's pulpit.

In all our conversations, I never heard him criticize or gossip about anyone. It has been said that there are two professions where jealousy is great. One is the "oldest" and medicine is the other. I later learned that there were those in the medical world, who, for various reasons, did not approve of my father, but he was always kind in his remarks about his colleagues. Also, I don't remember his ever criticizing me in our talks and this is unusual. He was much more interested in guiding me in the right direction.

I recall that when I was eleven years old, he was writing a book on arteriosclerosis (hardening of the arteries). In this book are many of his medical theories, some dealing with the aging process, which, of course, I did not understand at the time, some of them turned out to be almost prophetic as I look back on them today. He tried to impart some of this to me in our conversations.

My father was ahead of his time with regard to exercise. He thought heart disease could be prevented or even cured by exercise. He wrote: "Exercise is of prime importance in the prevention and treatment of arteriosclerosis. It is important to have specific instructions in what kind of exercise to take. Walking is the most available and generally satisfactory exercise." He often recommended that if one worked, say, on Wall Street, that one walk several stops before getting on the subway. He also thought that walking in the morning is more beneficial than at night.

Walking is a form of exercise I still prescribe today for my heart patients. Exercise in the prevention of heart disease is much discussed now, when joggers are a common sight on the streets of New York and all cities, large and small.

My father wrote a short piece called, "The Nine-Hole Cure for Heart Disease"—by playing nine holes of golf, you could accomplish a good deal in strengthening the heart and have fun besides. He was not sure how exercise benefited the heart, as we did not have then the sophisticated equipment available today to monitor a patient's progress. Actually, we are not sure

Mother and Father, c. 1925.

even today exactly why exercise is beneficial, but everyone agrees that it is.

He also talked to me a good deal about learning some sort of game. I did become a court game player, but he got me interested in fencing. He himself was a fencer and belonged to a fencing club. He thought that fencing was one of the best forms of exercise there is to develop yourself, a good exercise for the older person. In his book, he wrote: "Fencing has many advantages, particularly to the busy worker. A satisfactory amount of exercise, including a bath, can be obtained within an hour. Fencing exercises all the muscles without straining any of them. It steadies the nerves, quickens the eye and trains the temper." His ideas about exercise were in advance of the thinking of his time.

About the habits of individuals, about alcohol, I remember him saying very little. He drank only on occasion. I don't remember him talking in terms of abstinence, but rather moderation. I grew up totally unaware that there was such a thing as an alcoholic. I don't think I ever heard the subject discussed or any reference to any friends of the family as being such. At parties wine and champagne were served before dinner. In fact, I didn't have my first cocktail till I arrived at college in New Haven.

Alcohol was blamed for many things and, as far as arteriosclerosis was concerned, my father felt it was absurd to think it might be a causal factor. He felt that alcohol should be drunk as pure as possible and well-diluted. It should be taken in appropriate quantities with relation to food and, with these precautions, could cause no harm. He stated in his book: "Hence many drinkers, and of a cheerful disposition, escape arteriosclerosis, while using considerable quantities of good wine." This is as applicable today as it was then and a recent scientific study reports that individuals who take two drinks a day are less liable to have "heart attacks" than those who totally abstain. In other words, the chances of developing arteriosclerosis of the coronary arteries that supply the heart with blood is lessened.

My father did emphaze to me that drinking had other side effects that might be harmful, but I do not remember being warned about the possibility of addiction. Dr. Richard Cabot of Boston, in a paper published in the *Journal of the American Medical Association* in 1904, had written that he found no relationship between alcohol and arteriosclerosis, which I think influenced his thinking. He made the broad statement that he had never seen any medication or regimen, except general moderation, that influenced the development of arteriosclerosis. He felt that because alcohol, like many other things, can be abused, is no reason why it could not be properly used. He told me that if it becomes a habit, it is better to give it up entirely than to use it in moderation. This is what we know today in the management of alcoholics, and is generally accepted as fact. As far as the practicing physician is concerned, it is better not to advise alcohol at all.

His advice to me regarding tobacco was extremely realistic. He smoked a moderate number of cigars himself, and told me that, on general principles, a cigar is the least harmful form of smoking. A pipe is stronger, but is difficult to keep lit and, for that reason, does little harm. He felt that cigarettes are particularly harmful on account of the incomplete combustion and the frequency with which they are used. This is close to our present-day concept and could be told to any boy growing up today. This was, of course, before there was any knowledge of the relationship between tobacco and lung cancer. I was also told that in certain susceptible young people, the heart may become irritable and irregular, so that it was better not to use tobacco. He was well aware of the effect of nicotine, the active ingredient of tobacco.

As far as the management of arteriosclerosis was concerned, he did not feel tobacco had anything to do with its cause. He felt that it was a disadvantage and sometimes a great danger to certain people with arteriosclerosis to give up tobacco. I have noted in practice that when a patient voluntarily gives up his customary cigars or cigarettes, it can be an indication that his underlying condition has markedly worsened and might even be a warning of impending death.

We did not discuss medicine directly, because my medical schooling would come later, but I do remember that he was opposed to doctors giving prognoses, attempting to say how long a particular person with heart disease would live. He said "prognosis should be left to the prophets." He never gave a bad picture to a patient, but always held out hope—and he was the sort of man who engendered hope in the patient. Later, when I practiced with him, I could sense in patients, when they came to his office, that they felt he was a man who not only understood their heart problem, but would help them. Today, we know with more certainty that a patient's attitude can affect the course of the disease, according to the many psychiatric studies that have been done.

My father's life was so tied to medicine, that he rarely spoke of cultural things. I don't remember his discussing a book he thought I ought to read. He was very fond of the theatre. I became very much interested in the theatre because of this early exposure.

I don't remember his being interested in art. Opera did not interest him, or my mother, either. Dance or ballet was never mentioned.

These are subjects that I know I discussed with my father. I don't remember being told anything about sex. This was, of course, still the Victorian period, and sex was not easily discussed. My father seemed to take it for granted that I would learn about sex from my own contemporaries and this turned out to be the case.

My father had one dislike and that was of people sleeping late. This was often difficult for me, as I would go to late parties, and he never hesitated to get me up. He always said, "the best work

43

is done in the morning." He said that there was little worth-while work done after lunch and this appears true even today.

One point about my father is that he talked very little. People often commented how little he said. The fact was that, when-ever he did talk, he said something of importance. He did not engage in "small talk" or chatter, but he liked to listen. He might have seemed rude to some people, but it was just his way. Later on in life, he joined Rotary and became more outgoing but, when I was growing up, it seemed he spoke little, although he did speak freely to me. My mother likened him to an owl, in his looks, and he was considered a wise man.

The conversations I did have with my father would occur in rather strange places—sometimes on his boat, sometimes he would invite me to lunch with him somewhere. He was anxious to impart to me his philosophy of life.

Only recently, in reading Ruth Bennett's *Yours Faithfully: The Life of Louis Faugères Bishop, M.D.* (which was never pub-lished in its complete form), I discovered my father had kept letters that I had written to him at various times from school and college. Also included were postcards I had sent from East Hampton when my parents were in Europe. I don't think these letters add much to what I have said about my school days. They do emphasize to me that as an only son, I had a good relation-ship with my mother and father, which continued all of my life.

One letter written in December, now indicates to me that I was not a brilliant student. I wrote: "The exams are over and I am sorry to say I did badly on them. I don't know exactly why, but sometimes that happens. I am certainly looking forward to vacation, and we will have to start right in with our morning swims." (I used to swim at the New York Athletic Club early every morning when I was home for vacation. The Club was on 59th Street, where it still stands, near our house on 55th Street.) "As usual I have heard that you have been terribly busy." (As a boy I was always impressed with the amount of work my father did. I was not aware, I think, at this point in my life, of his great intellect.) "I am enclosing my chemistry exam which only 12 out of 50 passed in the Form. What I got is considered good though not passing. It was a very stiff exam. What do you think you could have gotten on it?" (I didn't realize at this point that chemistry would be a study problem for many years to come.) "I understand that at the end of the year I will be pretty well prepared for college, but if I want to pass Geometry I will have to do a little work at Christmas. We will talk this over." (My father wanted me to miss the sixth form, the final year, and enter college a year before my class. In later years, I have often

The second clubhouse, built on Sixth Avenue and Central Park South and opened in 1898, was reputed to be the most elegant and well appointed in the world. It furnished the backdrop for the NYAC's Golden Age.

wondered if this was a good idea.) "We have had two days of skating which was great." (Ice comes early in Concord, New Hampshire, one of the coldest spots in the world.) "I have been drilling about three times a week, so you see I have been busy." (The school felt it was only a question of time before we would be in the war, and they were right.) "There is a good deal of talk about the war, and there have been various lectures which I wrote to you about, but I don't think the fellows have realized how serious it is." (I must have thought I was the only boy that knew anything.) "I am looking forward to coming home a lot."

(I can understand this because home was a lot different than at St. Paul's).

Another letter written from Yale in 1919 illustrates some of my problems at this time. I don't think it very different from a letter one would write at that point in time: "Dear Father, After getting a Warning in math," (a warning meant you were not doing well in your studies) "I settled down to work hard, and have had good results including 100 in a Math Exam, which is unusual for me. I have been fencing in the afternoons and there is a lot of work to be done about the Team as I want to get the job of Manager next year." (This I eventually did get.) "I will probably come down next Saturday and will arrange to get together for some fun." (I always liked to be with my father.) "I have started in keeping a diary consisting of a few lines a day as you suggested of interesting things that happen, people you meet, etc." (This suggestion of my father I have kept up a good part of my life, even to the present time.) "I will need some more money to pay Brand bill etc. I have kept pretty careful track of everything I have spent, and if you do this you don't spend nearly as much. Although college is not a cheap proposition. Will you deposit $100 and I will send you statement of bills."

Later in life, I remember his discussing with me that, if anything happened to him, I must take care of my mother. Actually, she lived a long time after he died, and I tried to see that she was always comfortable and that I was close, if she needed me.

My father died in 1941 and, the last year of his life, he kept a small diary. The last entry before he died brought home to me the closeness of our relationship, which had always existed. The entry was, "L.F.B., Jr. W.O.R. 9-15—9:30 a.m." I was going to give a radio talk and he wanted to remember to listen. Up to the very end of his life, he continued to be interested in everything I did. He was always there to help me, if he could.

Chapter III

The Only Child

I AM SURE THAT MY MOTHER wanted more than one child, as it is unusual for most women to be satisfied with only one. When I asked her about this, my mother made the point that she was completely satisfied with me. But it is quite evident that the only child growing up in a family has problems that are not present when there are siblings.

The only child is the center of attention. There is no competition. The give and take that is part of growing up with other brothers and sisters is not there. Parents hope that the school environment will remedy this, and it does to some extent, but nevertheless, when he comes home, he is still the main attraction.

There is always the possibility that he will be spoiled.

The education of an only child is different; he is more exposed to adults. He is usually taken along wherever his parents go because there are no brothers or sisters to play with at home. As a result, he may hear a lot of adult conversation, which he may or may not understand.

In my own case, I also had an early introduction to theatre, which my family enjoyed. Had they liked music, I would have had an early education in music.

The only child is given the best of what a family can afford. There are no ''hand-me-downs.'' He may grow up with the feeling that this will go on forever. The question arises whether this causes a degree of selfishness or may cause problems later in life.

There is the other side of the coin. The only child feels he must give back what he is getting in his devotion to his mother and father, and this creates a sense of responsibility he may carry with him all of his life. He will not realize it when he is young but, in time, as he sees his parents growing old, he realizes that they depend on him to look after them, as there are no other children to share the responsibility.

An only child does have a closer relationship with parents,

because their attention is not shared with other siblings.

There has been a somewhat limited study of the only child by psychologists. A review of these studies appeared in the *Journal of Individual Psychology*, Vol. 33, May, 1977, Number 1. It was entitled "The Only Child: A Review," and written by Toni Falbo of the University of Texas at Austin. I was interested in how the studies applied to me.

The only child has an IQ advantage over children from large families. I never took an IQ test so I can't know if this applies to me, but, thinking about my academic life, I was never at the top of the class and usually in the middle.

There is a general opinion, borne out by research, that the only child achieves more than when there are numerous children. As far as I am concerned, this too is difficult to answer.

There is much interest in the question of achievement and a Carnegie study found that status, not brains, makes a child's future. "Given the compounding penalty of being poor, or a member of a racial minority or to parents of little education and with intermittent or dead-end employment, a particular child will be unlikely to advance significantly above the socio-economic status of the parents." The Horatio Alger situation is rare.

In my own case, my family was in good financial circumstances, although not rich. They were well-educated and would be considered WASPS in today's terminology.

I agree that the "acquisition of adult behavior is probably accelerated in only children because they have solely adult models of behavior in their family environment."

It is said that "the mother interacts with an only child twice as much as when there are other children." This may be bad. In my own case, I think it did no harm, as my father played an equal, if not more important, part in my growing up.

It has been reported that only children have fewer friends and belong to fewer clubs. This was not true in my own case. I think I have had the normal amount of friends in my lifetime, perhaps because I played games, and, if anything, I have often thought that I belonged to too many clubs.

With regard to the mental health of an only child, there is a popular conception that an only child is generally "maladjusted, self-centered and self-willed, attention seeking, and dependent on others, temperamental and anxious, generally unhappy and unlikeable." I hope I am not any of these, but one cannot judge one's self.

Chapter IV

St. Bernard's School

MY MOTHER THOUGHT THAT THE ONLY good education for a young boy was to be had at an English school. I remember that there was even talk about sending me to Eton. Later, I met men whose families had sent them to Eton, and there remains in New York an Old Etonian Society.

There did exist, in this country, preparatory schools, such as the Fay School, which to some extent copied the early forms of the British schools, where a boy might be sent before going off to a final boarding school. This meant that a boy left home at an early age and spent a good part of the year at school. Many, including my mother, considered this the best form of upper-class education.

At a dinner party, my mother met John C. Jenkins, who, with his partner, Francis H. Tabor, had started an English School here in New York called "St. Bernard's." These two young Englishmen had been educated at Cambridge; their aim was to apply the best features of an English public school to the needs of American boys. In other words, these boys would get the same discipline, learn the same sports, get the same education as if they were at Eton or Harrow.

Jenkins and Tabor were joint headmasters of the school, and it was a relationship that lasted from 1904 until October, 1925 when Mr. Tabor died of a stroke, while playing golf. By then, it had become one of New York's best known private schools, which it is to this day.

I went to St. Bernard's from 1908 until 1913. The school was located at 570 Fifth Avenue, between 46th and 47th Streets. It was over a well-known florist of the day called, I believe, Thorley. There were only two classrooms. Mr. Jenkins taught in one and Mr. Tabor in the other. Between them, they taught the subjects they thought young boys should learn. I was then seven years old.

Mr. Jenkins taught Latin, French, geography and mathematics. Mr. Tabor taught history, English and literature. At other

St. Bernard's at 570 Fifth Avenue, above Flower Shop.

schools, subjects such as Latin, French and English history would not have been considered at that level.

The two headmasters were completely different. Mr. Jenkins was the disciplinarian. One method he would use to keep a boy awake and alert was to fire an eraser at the boy's head.

Homework would be put on the blackboard and there would be no excuse for not getting it down correctly. There was also a preparatory period, when you could do your homework at the school from four to six in the afternoon.

When I first started at the school, Mary Smith would bring me and call for me. I was not allowed to go alone, although it was not a long walk from our house on 55th Street down Fifth Avenue to the school.

Roller skating was a favorite activity at that time, much as it is today. Also, in the afternoons, we were taken up to the Bronx, where we had the use of a field called the Berkeley Oval, where we were introduced to the English game of soccer. Both Jenkins and Tabor were fine players, and were able to teach the game to us. In the spring, we played baseball like all other American boys and there was an annual track meet that was held somewhere on Staten Island.

In learning and playing games, we were introduced to the English concept of sportsmanship. The English have been credited with developing the code of sportsmanship. We were taught to lose gracefully and not to take unfair advantage of an opponent. The English public schools had developed this "code" in the nineteenth century and, so important did our headmasters consider it, that Mr. Tabor had written a song about it:

THE SPORTMAN'S SONG

Today I play at soccer,
For summer's fun is fled,
And take from out my locker
My shirt of white and red;
Anon, when baseball calls me
All in my red and white,
Whatever else befalls me,
I play with all my might.

Francis Tabor (left) *and John Card Jenkins.*
Headmasters, St. Bernard's School.

I never seem to make a team,
My name's unknown to fame;
The captain's list my name has
missed,
Yet still I play the game.

And when the playfields spurning,
My soul to study turns,
To light the lanes of learning
My lamp at midnight burns
And with a will compelling
I learn to calculate,
To write and read with spelling
And verbs to conjugate.

CHORUS

Yet though I sip from scholarship
No taste of honey'd fame,
No triumphs scored on honour board,
Yet still I play the game.

These young schoolmasters were concerned with developing character and they felt that playing close contact sports was one way to further this. It recalls the words of Wellington: "The Battle of Waterloo was won on the playing fields of Eton."

Whereas Mr. Jenkins (or Jenks, as he was called) taught in the formal manner, Mr. Tabor had more unorthodox methods. During our English literature period, he would quote and sing much of Gilbert and Sullivan. One of his interests was the Boys Club in Tompkins Square on the lower East Side of New York, where he became director. There he trained a group of boys in a Gilbert and Sullivan operetta each year.

Someone recently wrote, "Where would the English language be today but for the ministrations of W. S. Gilbert? We'd probably all be speaking to one another in the language of Tennyson and putting each other to sleep. Instead we sing along and speak along at performances of *The Mikado*".

This early exposure to Gilbert and Sullivan remains with me today. Many people I know dislike or are bored by Gilbert and Sullivan, but I can only think that they were not exposed to their work, as we were. It is gratifying to me that young people of today flocked to *The Pirates of Penzance* on Broadway and enjoyed it.

Tabor would not only quote the lyrics, but could sit down at the piano and play and sing the wonderful Sullivan melodies.

St. Bernard's, c. 1910.

Sports Day at St. Bernard's. The High Jump, Headmaster Jenkins.

In thinking about Tabor, who had come to America from Corpus Christi College, Cambridge, I am reminded of one of the great lines from *H. M. S. Pinafore*, "But in spite of all temptations to belong to other nations, he remained an Englishman."

Although we did not realize it at the time, we were being taught the English language. No other composer has made us aware of the beauty of words, at the same time, employing wit and merriment.

Mr. Tabor's unique way of teaching extended to poetry, which he also read to us or had us memorize. It was his idea, as expressed by Arthur Quiller-Couch in his preface to *The Oxford Book of English Verse 1250–1900*, to "implant the love of poetry in some young minds not yet initiated," and so it was with us. I am sure that this is so, because all of my life I have read from time to time the works of the great poets, although not always understanding their meaning.

Tabor taught us that, for the most part, poetry told a story. His favorite poet was Sir Walter Scott and he liked particularly "The Lady of the Lake." We could all quote the first two lines of this narrative poem:

> *The stag at eve had drunk his fill,*
> *Where danced the moon on Monan's rill.*

We were also greatly impressed with Scott's great patriotic poem with the opening lines:

> *Breathes there the man, with soul so dead,*
> *Who never to himself hath said,*
> *This is my own, my native land!*

It was also what one would expect of an English schoolmaster that we were filled up with Shakespeare. Before I left the school, we were actually performing some of Shakespeare's plays but, in the early days they were read to us.

We were told to see, when we could, the great Shakespearian performers of the day. The two I best remember at that time were Julia Marlowe and E. H. Sothern. On the Broadway stages, there were no more cultivated or dedicated performers of Shakespeare than these two. It is said of their *Macbeth* that it was their finest work and Julia Marlowe's sensual Lady Macbeth was not only original for its time, but her masterpiece.

In my second or third year at the school, Mr. Tabor produced a play called *Vice Versa*, in which I had a small part, but I had become so interested in actually being on a stage that I had memorized all the parts. We were to do the play before the families and friends of St. Bernard's. About a week before we were to do the play, the boy playing the leading role became sick. This was a boy called Yale Kneeland, who in later life went on to become one of the leading physicians in the United States. I was chosen to step into the part, following the theatre tradition that "the show must go on" and that other theatre tradition about the unknown becoming a star. While not getting a star on my dressing room door, I was later presented with a gold penknife for my efforts.

During my schooldays at St. Bernard's, my parents often took me to the theatre. Our evening was usually preceded by a table d'hote dinner, which in this day and age has the elegant name of *prix fixe* or, as many restaurants call it, "pre-theatre" dinner. Dinner, including wine, was at a set price. It was known as the "dollar dinner," which was exactly what it cost. My family liked an Italian restaurant called Gonfarone's best.

At the theatre, we usually sat in the balcony. $2.00 or $1.50 bought orchestra seats, and balcony seats were, of course, less, as they are today. Brooks Atkinson, in his book, *Broadway*, describes this first theatre decade of the twentieth century as "artistically trivial," but says that "it had charm and a kind of disarming simplicity."

I considered going to the theatre a wonderful adventure. Many of the niceties of theatre-going of that time have disappeared. All theatres had a pit orchestra that played musical selections before the show began, as well as during the intermission and after the final curtain. This custom is no longer with us; if there is any music at all, it is usually canned and unattractive.

I carefully preserved all the theatre programs from that time and later years but, unfortunately, they were destroyed some twenty years ago when our house in the country was flooded.

As a boy, my special idol was William Gillette, who introduced Sherlock Holmes to the American theatre, for which he was remembered as long as he lived. Recently his Civil War play, *Secret Service*, was revived in New York, some sixty years after he performed it.

Theatres were known for certain types of entertainment. One of my friends recently told me that her family would never discuss the name of the play they would be seeing, but simply would say that they were going to the Criterion or the Empire. The Empire, at Broadway and 39th Street, is the one that I remember.

Going to the Empire was a gala occasion. It was customary to dress in evening clothes, especially if you sat in the orchestra. The season often opened there, with John Drew appearing in a drawing-room comedy. I had heard about John Drew because they all lived down at East Hampton, where we spent summers. John Drew was considered quite a character there. When I was a young man, he was pointed out to me as a famous actor. He also took part in the summer resort scene. So, the Drew-Barrymore tradition was one of the early ones I grew up with.

The theatre district between 37th Street and 42nd Street was known as "the Rialto," and a common expression which I remember my mother using was, "What's new on the Rialto?" Broadway also had spectacular productions, such as "Ben

William Gillette as Sherlock Holmes.

Hur'', where a chariot race was recreated on stage.

Later on, as a young man, I continued to go to the theatre, whenever I could, either alone or with friends. There was an institution known as Gray's Drugstore. I suppose it had the usual things a drugstore would carry, but in addition, all the theatres sent their unsold tickets to Gray's, where they would be auctioned off, as it were, before the performance, at reduced rates. It was a fun and cheap way to go to the theatre, if you were willing to wait, for you never knew what you would see. As a young man, I was not that discriminating, as long as it was theatre. The scene at Gray's before curtain time resembled the Stock Exchange on a busy day. A second method was to buy standing room seats, and often you could find a seat once the curtain went up.

Growing up in New York meant that from an early age on, I was exposed to theatre and to opera, which I think added much to my education.

The attempts by Mr. Tabor to initiate us into the theatre was a further broadening. I might say, that from that point on, a love of the theatre was instilled in me, present to this day, and I then strongly considered being an actor when I grew up.

Mr. Jenkins taught the subjects we thought least interesting but, nevertheless, we admired and respected him as a man; and that is very important to a schoolboy.

He taught us Latin, from the Latin textbook *Ritchie's First Steps*. Latin was taught in all English schools and was considered vital to an educated man. Later on, at St. Paul's, my father insisted that I also study Greek.

The teachings of our schoolmasters extended beyond the classroom. We were expected to behave like civilized gentlemen. I recall one winter afternoon when Mary Smith, who usually called for me, failed to come. Mr. Tabor invited me to wait in his rooms, which were above the school. I watched as he proceeded to dress for dinner, as did all upper class Englishmen. He was aided by a valet, the "gentleman's gentleman." I noticed that Mr. Tabor smoked a pipe, which he never did at school. He offered me a glass of sherry, as a host might. He treated me as a guest and, for that brief time, there seemed no age difference.

When I was finally called for, I felt very grown-up, for I had glimpsed this special adult world where gentlemen dressed for dinner. I had sipped sherry, but more importantly, been treated not as a schoolboy, but as a visitor. No doubt, this was a further extension of my education for it would not have been characteristic of an American school, but was unique to St. Bernard's.

Before I left school, it had increased in size and reputation and moved up to East 60th Street, where it occupied a brownstone front. New schoolmasters from England were added, all of whom played an important role in the development of the school.

There was no official graduation. At a certain point, you merely took off for boarding school. In my case, at thirteen, I was enrolled at St. Paul's. Most of St. Bernard's boys went either to St. Paul's, Groton or St. Mark's. Such was the reputation of St. Bernard's, that those boys who went there were readily accepted at boarding schools.

St. Bernard's is now on East 98th Street and, in 1981, you might say I came full circle, for I had the pleasure of addressing the senior students on the work of Oliver Wendell Holmes, the physician and poet. They seemed to me a fine group of boys, more mature at fourteen than I had anticipated, really almost young adults.

I might say, as I watched the younger boys in the halls and sensed the energy and activity, it brought back memories of two classrooms over Thorley's seventy-three years before.

DANCING SCHOOL

Before I went to boarding school, my mother sent me to dancing school. There was only one in New York at the time that had any real social significance; it was called Dodsworth's. This was a famous school of dancing and existed from 1835 until 1920. When I went to Dodsworth's, it was run by George Dodsworth, a nephew of Allan Dodsworth, who had first opened the school.

The Dodsworth's that I went to carried on many of the traditions of the original. The gilded age of the Gay Nineties, with its great wealth and extravagance, had ushered in a complete change in the dancing school picture. Because of the chaotic state of the dance during the First World War period, The New York Society of Teachers of Dancing was formed in the spring of 1914, and George Dodsworth became the first president. A history of American social ballroom dancing calls this period, when I was taking lessons, the "Society Era."

Dodsworth's had the reputation for being the place to send a boy, particularly if you were a socially ambitious mother, which most mothers were. I don't know whether this played a role in my case but, in any event, dutifully dressed in a blue suit, patent leather shoes and gloves, I went there once a week. Honestly, I don't think any boy who went enjoyed it.

George Dodsworth had a large house on East 49th Street, containing a ballroom large enough to contain his classes, which usually took place in the afternoon. Mr. Dodsworth was tall and, of course, always well-dressed. We were taught the rudiments of dancing, but part of our training was to learn manners, the social graces, etiquette and deportment.

When you arrived, you would bow to Mr. Dodsworth and to the waiting girls and then sit on the side of the room reserved for the boys. The girls would sit on the other side and Mr. Dodsworth would stand in the center to illustrate the dances we were learning. There was a pianist and a violinist accompanying.

We were taught group dances, such as the "Cotillion" and the "Lancers" and round dances, such as the waltz and the polka, which was a sort of sliding step where you had to jump and click your heels together. The new "Two-step" was not yet taught. Later, in the ragtime era, would come the so-called "animal dances," such as the "Bunny Hug' and the "Turkey Trot."

Mr. Dodsworth had one custom and that was, when you were not too clumsy and managing to traverse the floor, however awkwardly, you were given a blue ribbon, as an indication of making progress in your dancing career. I can't remember the name of any boy or girl in the dancing class and this must be because I, as did many other boys, went reluctantly.

When I was older, and at St. Paul's, these social graces were put to use, for I found myself invited to subdeb dances, given for girls before they "came out" or were formally presented to society. These dances were usually held at the Colony Club or at the old Ritz-Carlton Hotel. They were run by committees, or what were called "patronesses," whose function it was to see that the children attended who "belonged." These dances had names such as "The Colony," and "The Metropolitan." There were lists of boys who were attending St. Paul's, Groton, St. Mark's and other prep schools considered "correct." I think I was on the list for one or two of these dances, but often I would be invited to go with one of the Emmet girls, sisters of Christy Emmet, my great friend at St. Paul's.

The parents of many of the girls would invite you to dine before the dance. This would insure that their daughters would have dancing partners. Dress was usually "black tie." The full dress suit or "tails" was not required until we reached the debutante period.

There were always more boys than girls at these dances, necessitating what was called a "stag line." The stag line usually consisted of 60 boys, sort of huddled in the center of the floor, around whom the couples danced. You would dart out, accost a pair and "cut in" by tapping the boy partner on the shoulder, signalling him to relinquish his girl partner to you. There would be no protracted conversation with the young lady, just a comment on the party, sometimes nothing. The object was just to keep moving. A popular girl would dance only a few steps with any one boy. You would be stuck with an unpopular girl unless you could prevail on one of your friends to relieve you. This was a cruel system.

The whole experience was a completely asexual one, for the girls were closely chaperoned. In our "liberated" era today, this whole picture would be considered ridiculous.

There was not supposed to be any drinking at these subdeb dances, but there were occasions when the punch would be "spiked" with hard liquor. Supper was always served at midnight and never varied: creamed chicken, peas and ice cream. The dance continued for a time after supper, until the orchestra played "Good Night, Ladies," and it was time to go home.

Chaperones or parents would come for the girls to take them home. A few affluent ones had their cars and chauffeurs.

It was rather a closed society, but it was my introduction to the social world.

Chapter V

St. Paul's School

ST. PAUL'S SCHOOL, which is in Concord, New Hampshire, is a church school, dedicated to "the education of the Christian scholar and gentleman." My father had gone there before me, and I had grown up with the tradition that I would eventually be a "St. Paul's Boy" or "Paulee" as they are called now.

I did not know at the time that I would never graduate from this school, but would leave in order to get a "quick start" in my future career in medicine.

I have a number of recollections of the school at that period, very much the same as some of the thoughts of J. Lawrence Barnard, another "St. Paul's Boy", in his book, *Gently Down the Stream*. I was a student some eleven years before the period he describes. I tried to have lunch with him to compare my notes about St. Paul's with his but, unfortunately, he died shortly after the publication of his book.

St. Paul's School, when I attended, was under the rectorship of Dr. Samuel S. Drury, who was considered one of the great schoolmasters of his time. Dr. Drury was called "The Drip." I had been told that he was called "The Drip" because he had preached a sermon where he had said, "The rain went drip, drip, drip." Dr. Drury became famous for his sermons, and many of them have been published.

As I remember him, he was a very unapproachable man. I had very little to do with him, except for one final occasion, before I left the school. It was not a particularly pleasant one. At the end of my fifth form year, I told him that I was going to go to Rosenbaum's Tutoring School and would not be returning as a sixth former. He did not approve of this. He handed me a Bible to take with me and sternly told me that I was not doing the right thing. I remember that I did not get any encouragement.

My second form year, my first year at the school, was the first time I had been away from home and, needless to say, I had the usual homesickness, which eventually every boy gets over.

Despite the fact that most of the boys who came to St. Paul's School at that time came from comfortable and luxurious back-

St. Paul's, the Lower School, c. 1914.

grounds, as second formers they led a very spartan existence. The lower school, where the second form resided, was presided over by Dr. Brinley. I remember that he was a friend of my father's. He seemed to me a kindly man, very different from "The Drip."

We lived in a long, high-ceilinged room, partitioned into cubicles or alcoves, about twenty down each side, with windows in the air space above the partitions. These alcoves were just big enough for a cot, a bureau, a small table and a camp chair; this was spartan simplicity, to say the least. Privacy was furnished by a curtain at the open end. There was also a wash basin. We were later to learn that, in the winter, the water in the basin would freeze and it would be necessary to break the ice to wash in the morning. One night was designated as "bath night," when one would take a bath.

I soon learned that it was important to be a good athlete at St. Paul's in the sports that were played there, which consisted in the fall of football and hockey, in neither of which I was proficient.

Early in the fall, I saw for the first time the famous St. Paul's "black ice." The water in the main body of water becomes hardened four or five feet thick and is crystal clear, black, glossy and hard. I have never heard of this anywhere else, but it is probably a well-known phenomena in New England.

I was also to learn how cold it is at St. Paul's. This became evident in many ways: your hair would freeze when you went

outdoors, as well as the frozen ice in the wash basin. Years later, when my son was serving in Germany near the Russian front, he was accosted by a Russian, who spoke some English, and he said to my son, "This is a very cold night here." My son replied, "You, sir, have never been to St. Paul's!"

Shortly after starting the fall term, I found myself in the choir. This was totally unexpected, as I never could carry a tune. Nevertheless, I was chosen. The choir in those days was under a famous choirmaster and musician, whose name was Knox. We rehearsed at least one night a week. Of course, I wore the

The Chapel, St. Paul's School.

choirboy's regalia and took an active part in all chapel cere-
monies. We had to go to chapel every morning and twice on
Sundays. Being a member of the choir introduced me to some
of the great church music at an early age. Mr. Knox had us
singing many of the famous anthems. Although I had little confidence in my singing ability, I did greatly enjoy being a part of
the choir.

The most well-known anthem to all St. Paul's boys is "Oh,
Pray for the Peace of Jerusalem." The words have stayed with
me all my life. A few years ago, while attending a medical congress in Israel, the congress was opened by this same prayer. I
was sitting next to an orthodox Jewish doctor friend of mine
from New York, and he was totally surprised when I repeated
the words. He said, "Where did you learn that?" Later on, we
toured Jerusalem together, and when we returned to New York,
he wrote to me telling me that he had greatly enjoyed being with
me, and he ended up his letter by saying, "You are a good Jew,"
which I considered a high compliment.

One of the advantages of choir practice is that it got a boy out
of study. There was also what was known as a "choir holiday." All holidays were, of course, welcome from our confined
environment.

CHRISTMAS VACATION

Christmas vacation was an important event at St. Paul's School
and, except for a very few boys who lived too far away, everyone went home. There was a special train that went directly
from Concord to New York. The arrival at Grand Central Sta-
tion was a social event.

On this particular day, we would all get up early and breakfast always included steak. It was generally thought that the
reason for this was that we would carry home a good impression of the food at the school. In my day, if there was snow on
the ground, and there usually was, we would be driven into
Concord in sleighs.

Besides the plays I might see during vacation, I always looked
forward to two entertainment institutions that existed in New
York at the time. One was the Hippodrome, and the other, the
Palace. The Hippodrome was at 43rd Street and Sixth Avenue,
in the shadow of the sixth Avenue El. The Hippodrome has been
described as being a triumph of showmanship. It seated 5,000
people. At every performance the chorus girls marched out of
sight into a tank, giving the illusion of a mass drowning. The
Hippodrome was not to be missed!

Sarah Bernhardt leaving her private railroad car with her manager, Edward J. Sullivan, 1911. **(The New York Public Library)**

I also never missed the show at the Palace. Vaudeville was at its height and to "play the Palace" meant you ad reached the top. Besides the best comedians and singing acts, magicians were likely to appear there (I had become very interested in magic). Circus and animal acts also appeared.

One of my recollections of the Palace is when Sarah Bernhardt was booked there. Everyone went to see her but all I remember is that she had a beautiful voice, although she spoke in French and I didn't understand a word she said. I was later told that she received five hundred dollars in gold from the management before every performance. I understand payment in gold to performers is again customary today.

Our family Christmas celebration never varied from year to year. Because we had a German background, the main event took place on Christmas Eve. Usually, when I arrived from school, preparation had already begun for my mother's big party. In addition to the family, there were friends invited, especially those who had no family of their own.

There was always a large decorated tree. Just as in the country, where one can cut down a tree of one's choice, in New York at Christmas one can buy any one from the great truckloads of trees that come down from Maine or Canada. I was always at home in time for the decorating of the tree, an event that took place a few days before the party. Only a few close friends were invited to help out, but it was really another small party in preparation for the big one. As is everyone's custom, Christmas decorations for the tree were preserved from past years and a few new ones were added. There was always a star on the top, accompanied by a big angel.

The ornaments included jewel-colored balls, little glass birds and small angels, which were all easily attached. Lit candles were used, but I don't remember that we ever had a fire.

My mother would have a present for everyone. Each present would be carefully wrapped and placed under the tree to be distributed at the party. The character of the party never changed and was carried on all of my mother and father's lives. I am indebted to my daughter, Anne, for a description of one such party, written many years later, in an essay called, "My Grandfather." It was no different from the time when I was a boy. This is how she told it:

"After every guest had arrived, we went into dinner, which was held in the living room and library. (The dining room was not large enough in the apartment my mother and father lived in.) It was customary for Grandma and Grandpa to sit at the head of the table in the big living room. In the library were seated the younger members of the family and their friends. At each place was a song sheet and on it were all of the old-time favorites. During the dinner, the man who helped Grandma and Grandpa run the parties would call out the name of a certain song, and we would sing it. (The favorite Christmas song my mother loved was the German one, 'O Tannenbaum, O Tannenbaum.' Grandma invariably hired the same musicians, two black men, whom she engaged every Christmas Eve for a number of years."

Everyone was required to dress and, in my day, that meant

that the men wore dress suits and the ladies long dresses, as well as all the jewels they might possess. In later years, there was less formality, but the party took place year after year, pretty much as my daughter described it.

During the long dinner, there would be many toasts and speeches. My father had a great love for Rutgers, his *alma mater*. The inside of his dress coat was lined with scarlet (the Rutgers color), and he always sang the Rutgers song, accompanied by the musicians, which begins "On the banks of the old Raritan." It always had a profound effect on me and may be why I have always felt that identification with something, in this instance a college, was important and should be carried on through one's life.

My mother loved the theatre and, in later years, we always had a Christmas play. Although I do not remember it as a boy, no doubt it took place. The play never varied from year to year. It was, of course, the old Christmas story. It was again well described by Anne in her school essay:

"Barbara (my sister) and I usually took the part of angels or shepherds and Grandpa and Grandma chose a woman guest to be the Virgin. This was an important decision, and they debated long and seriously before they made a final decision. My mother was chosen practically every time, but when she was not well enough or too busy someone else was given the part."

Actually, my wife was often pregnant, which did not seem to make any difference. I'm afraid that none of us ever learned our lines very well, and there were many hesitations and frequent promptings. Angels wandered in at the wrong time and there were crashes backstage and various interruptions. However no one seemed to mind, and we always said the performance was better than the year before!

GAMES

Moving up from the lower school at St. Paul's we were moved to a similar environment, but in another building. It was soon evident to me that I would not distinguish myself as an athlete at St. Paul's.

For sports such as football, hockey and baseball (which as a matter of fact wasn't played very much), there were three clubs, which everyone automatically joined: Isthmian, Delphian and Old Hundred. You belonged to one of these clubs and played for it in any sport you happened to take part in. Because my father had been Isthmian, I joined the Isthmian Club and represented it in the little I did in sports. The inter-club system is a good one, because it gives everyone a chance to play for a specific club and to represent it.

While attending St. Bernard's, I had played baseball and soccer, and played these games reasonably well, I thought, until I went to boarding school, where the standards were much higher. I soon also found out that I was no good at the so-called "contact" sports, such as football and hockey, which were the main fall and winter games. 1 was equally bad at rowing and track, which took place in the spring. I tried both of these without success. At one time I thought I was a high jumper but, at St. Paul's, I was outclassed in competition.

The only "letter" I got was a hat for squash racquets, with "Isthmian" on the brim of the hat. The very good athletes got sweaters with the club names on them. I was never fortunate enough to get one of these.

About that time, I met a boy who was to become one of my lifelong friends. His name was Christopher Emmet. His friendship during those years had a great influence on me. I knew nothing about his family and his artistic background, but only that we seemed to have a lot in common.

He convinced me that there were things to pursue other than football and hockey and that one could play other games, in particular, squash racquets and golf, both of which he played. I did not know at that time that his family had a private squash court at his home in Long Island. With Christy's help, I devoted myself to becoming a good squash player at St. Paul's.

St. Paul's had been given a number of courts, which gave me the opportunity to play. I not only found that I loved the game, but that I was good at it. As a boy, I never thought it would play a big part in my later life, because it was, at the time, a relatively unknown game. No one foresaw the future of this game, now played all over the United States. During college, I gave up squash and concentrated on fencing but, when I was in medical school, I was again to find my true love, court games, which I played until I suffered an injury to my knee in my middle fifties.

In my fourth form year, I moved into what was then called the "20" house. There, for the first time, I had a room and a roommate. I considered this very luxurious. My roommate was a boy named Wigglesworth. The name seemed a bit peculiar, but I later learned that this was a very distinguished Boston family name. We got along well, although he was the exact opposite from me, as he was an outstanding St. Paul's athlete. Later, he became "stroke" of what I recall was the Halcyon crew. There were two main boat clubs at St. Paul's, one called Shadduck and the other Halcyon. Rowing was one of the other great sports at St. Paul's in which I never took any part.

One of the unpleasant things I recall was the practice of "hazing." One of the bigger boys, Marburg by name, came from a celebrated Baltimore family. He was particularly unpleasant to me and I developed a real dislike of him, which continued for many years after I left school. Years later, at a reunion of our class, I found him a most attractive, delightful man. It was hard for me to remember my early feelings. Time brings many changes. When you are young, it is easy to hurt someone. At school, I had made up my mind that if I ever saw him again, I would smack him in the nose.

Also, at one of the reunions, I discovered that my old roommate, Wigglesworth, had become a poet, which seemed a very unlikely career at the time we roomed together.

HORATIO ALGER, SUMMER VACATIONS AND WAR

I was brought up on the stories of Horatio Alger. There is still a Horatio Alger awards committee, a nonprofit corporation which gives awards to those who have followed the Horatio Alger tradition. Individuals who have pulled themselves up by their bootstraps and worked their way up in the world by various menial jobs are selected. All have become famous people.

As we had Sunday brunch at The Piping Rock Club recently, I wondered how many older members fitted this concept. An English friend of mine stated that there is no such thing in England and that the "rags to riches" story is rare there. Today, in America, "Horatio Alger" is part of our language. It is used to signify spectacular rise to fame and success. Usually it is one who started from scratch, against great odds, and reached the top of the ladder.

I have always wondered whether I might have been cheated by not having had this challenge. Friends have told me frequently how they sold newspapers and earned their school tuition waiting on tables. These appear to be the most usual occupations, although there no doubt were others. In my family, at any rate, it never was even suggested that I should do any work while I was growing up. In fact, quite the opposite was true. Both in summer and winter, my education was what was important.

In the winter, I went first to the best private nursery school, then called, as it is now, "kindergarten," and later to St. Bernard's and, finally, to St. Paul's. In the summer, a logical time for boys to seek some sort of work, the thought was never entertained. Quite the opposite happened. When I was quite young, the family went up to York Harbor, Maine, where my father practiced and I played on the beach under careful supervision. Later, we went to Easthampton, as popular a resort then as it is now. There I did all the things young boys do in a summer resort. There was a boys club, where we were supervised as a group, and our activities included several overnight camping trips.

None of this was as much fun for me as golf and tennis. Easthampton had a beautiful club, the Maidstone, where all of this was possible and I took full advantage. I don't think, in those days, the professionals taught young boys as they do today in many clubs, but it was possible to play with others and to learn the games. There were tournaments that attracted some of the best players in the country.

We also swam in the pool and the ocean.

I was encouraged to do all these things, which I now realize was at great expense to my family, but it was never suggested that I had to work for these privileges. I also never gave a thought to the cost of equipment, such as tennis racquets and balls, golf clubs, bathing suits and all the other equipment needed for sports, which were paid for without question.

During summer holiday, when I was growing up, I did attend a lot of Broadway musicals. I recall very well the old Princess Theatre, which actually seated very few people. It was here that Jerome Kern had his first successes. I saw them all. These included, "Oh, Boy," "Leave It to Jane" and "Oh, Lady, Lady," to name a few. I was entranced by Kern's music and, although I had no musical ability or training, I did enjoy it very much and it made an impression on me at that time.

There was also the "Follies," which we saw nearly every year. The genius of Florenz Ziegfield was evident to every boy growing up. The "Follies" were the most glamorous series of shows that Broadway ever had and, I think, ever will have. Ziegfield glorified beautiful girls in a way that no one else has emulated. Among them were Marion Davies, Peggy Hopkins Joyce, Mae Murray, Barbara Stanwyck, Paulette Goddard and Irene Dunne, who went on to successful careers. To this day, there is an organization of former "Ziegfield Girls" that meets and pursues good works.

Besides this, Ziegfield attracted the best composers for his shows, including Rudolf Friml and Irving Berlin. I still remember those early songs: "Hello, Frisco, Hello," which saluted the long-distance telephone, was sung by Ina Claire; Nora Bayes sang "Shine On, Harvest Moon"; Berlin's "A Pretty Girl is Like a Melody," which was first sung at the Follies, is still played and sung today.

Ziegfield also had a wonderful group of comedians: Bert Williams, W. C. Fields, Ed Wynn, Eddie Cantor, Fannie Brice, Will Rogers, to name a few.

The Follies were imitated in George White's "Scandals," Earl Carroll's "Vanities" and many other shows but, while these were successful, none captured the splendor, the magic of the Ziegfield "Follies."

When we didn't go to East Hampton, my family took me with them to Europe, particularly to Bad Nauheim in Germany. It was here that my father brought some of his patients, to get the benefit of this German cure (*Kur*), which devoted itself particularly to the heart patient.

My only interest at Bad Nauheim was to continue to play golf and tennis, which were available there also.

It was one of these trips abroad that I had my first experience of what war means when it strikes. My mother and father and myself, as well as several of his patients, were at Bad Nauheim, living at the Grand Hotel. (There was a "Grand Hotel" everywhere in Europe.) One day, all the help began leaving and the hotel was in chaos. We learned that the German Army had been ordered to mobilize, and that was the reason for the staff's departure. War between England and Germany was officially declared on August 1, 1914.

I was playing in a golf tournament with a German boy and we came in second. My German partner left before the prizes were awarded, and I came home with the Cup. On it was engraved:

GOLF

Bad Nauheim/August 1st, 1914
Mens Doubles/2nd Prize Won by L.F. Bishop, Jr.

The big question was how to get our party out of Germany. There would be difficulty with acceptance of our money for transportation. Among the patients my father had brought with him was Louis Swift, connected with the meat packing family. He had anticipated the crisis in advance, and had brought with him a suitcase filled with gold, which then as now is acceptable currency anywhere, under any circumstances. The letters of credit which everyone carried were of no value. I remember one other of my father's patients there, who had become very rich because of his invention of the "lollipop." He had a lollipop painted on his luggage for easy identification. However, gold was the currency of the day, and not lollipops.

Mr. Swift chartered a boat to take all the Americans there out of Germany. We went down the Rhine to Holland, where we got a steamer back to America. We came back on the Rotterdam, which was filled with Americans getting out of Europe. I would not return again to Europe until after I graduated from college and went on the so-called "Grand Tour."

My recollection of St. Paul's during my last term there is that some of our time was used to prepare for the war in which we might become involved.

World War I was being fought in the trenches and we were taught how to dig trenches and how to get in and out with a rifle in your hand. At that time, I did not realize that I would be part of a military training program the following fall at Yale.

Of course, many St. Paul's boys have fought in this country's wars. The names of St. Paul's boys who fought in 1861 are read aloud each year at a ceremony on Decoration Day, as well as those who fought in 1898, 1918, World War II, Korea and Vietnam.

Owen Wister calls attention to the statue near the edge of the lower pond in front of the library. It is a figure in military dress, which personifies "a boy in his hour of dedication, his choice made, his true soul visible."

My last year at St. Paul's was spent in the old Upper, which is no longer there. It was on a hill, overlooking the library pond. This was a rather austere building but, for the first time, I had a room to myself.

Often, insignificant things are what one remembers about school life. During the winter, one of the concoctions the boys drank was "brew." It was made by adding condensed milk to chocolate or cocoa and hot water and served in a crock or beer mug. It was a very popular afternoon drink that year.

LETTERS

After my mother's death, I found a batch of letters I had written home from St. Paul's School, which my mother had kept. These letters reflected my feelings and my activities as a student there. Reading these letters, I found out much about myself at age 14, away at school, that I had forgotten. I had learned early that I was not made for football or, for that matter, for the great school sport, hockey. I talked a good deal about the choir and choir practice and mention the name of an anthem, which seemed to have a significant title, "Arise, Arise and Shine for Thy Light Has Come."

I repeated what has impressed every St. Paul's boy, "It was awful cold in the dormitory the other night, but I have plenty of blankets." My interest in music was further apparent: "Will you please send me the Columbia Song Book for piano. You can get it at Ditson's on 34th Street. I want to do a little practicing on my mandolin before I come home." Ditson's was the famous music store of the time.

For the most part, these letters are no doubt what every boy writes home, in one form or another. One of the letters included the daily schedule, which is probably not much different now from what it was then:

7:00 Get up
7:30 Breakfast
8:10 Chapel
Morning study and from right after
lunch till 10 minutes to five to play
6:30 Supper
7:10 - 8:10 Study
8:10 - 9:05 You can read, study or write letters

The letters also reflect how important it was to get home for Christmas. Concord is a long way from New York when you are 14. I wrote: "It is only a little over 2 weeks before I start home (16 days)." One line in the letters expresses the feelings of all young boys when I wrote: "I got your nice letter today, and you bet, I don't want to change mothers."

ROSENBAUM'S

The following spring, I left St. Paul's for Rosenbaum's.

I have mixed emotions about not having finished the sixth form, which Dr. Drury had emphasized was a necessity. My father did not think so, but felt that by "tutoring" I could easily get into college the following fall.

The requirements for college admission were not as strict as they are today. It was only necessary to pass college examinations, have enough points and you were in!

In those days, there were three major tutoring schools, all of which more or less guaranteed to get you into college, no matter how dumb you were. One was run by the Rosenbaum family in Milford, Connecticut. There was also one called "The

Widow'' in Boston and one somewhere near Princeton. Rosenbaum's prepared you for Yale and that was where I wanted to go.

Rosenbaum's was really a unique place. Most of the boys who went there had been cast out of the various prep schools for one reason or another. Their families had given up hope of their getting into college and this was their last chance.

Two or three Rosenbaums ran the school. The school program involved intensive tutoring. The status of the school could be summed up in the first two lines of the school song which went:

> *Rosie's once, Rosie's twice,*
> *Holy, Jumping, Jesus Christ!*

Rosie's had very few failures and any boy going there was more or less assured of getting into Yale that fall. The reason was that they appeared to know exactly what would be asked on the entrance examinations. This was based on many years' experience.

Each student received personal attention. It was very intensive and I might say, very expensive. Only very privileged families could afford the tuition. My father's purpose in sending me there was that he thought I could skip a year and get into college earlier. He felt the cost was worth it.

One of the problems at Rosenbaum's was that some of the students drank to excess. I did not, so there was no problem as far as I was concerned, but the drinking at the school did interfere with the routine.

When fall arrived and, with it, the examinations, as expected, Rosie's had ''spotted'' most of the questions. As a result, I entered Yale with very high marks. I often wondered what became of this school. I believe that it later became the Milford Academy, a very respectable boys school.

It became apparent to me later that to have skipped the sixth form at St. Paul's had certain social disadvantages. You did not go to college with your schoolmates. You found yourself alone with no close friends.

Chapter VI

The Emmet Family

MY GREAT FRIEND AT ST. PAUL'S SCHOOL was Christopher Emmet and we remained friends throughout our adult lives. He taught me many things. The lament of the Greek poet, Callimachus, "Heraclitus," here paraphrased in a poem by William Johnson Cory, applies to him:

They told me, Heraclitus. They told me
you were dead.
They brought me bitter news to hear
and bitter tears to shed.
I wept, as I remembered, how often you
and I
Had tired the sun with talking and sent
him down the sky.
And now that thou art lying, my dear
old Carian guest,
A handful of grey ashes, long long ago
at rest,
Still are thy pleasant voices, thy
Nightingales, awake,
For Death, he taketh all away, but
them he cannot take.

Chris had the most attractive voice I have ever heard and as a young man a cultural knowledge that I greatly appreciated. As a result of our friendship, I was introduced into the Emmet family and, from then on, spent part of every summer with them. Their way of life was in complete contrast to anything I had known before.

They lived in a great rambling house in St. James, Long Island, overlooking the Sound, and it appeared that they had an enormous amount of property, which included private tennis and squash courts, which impressed me indeed. I had played squash at school, but it seemed incredible to me that anyone could have his own private court.

Mr. and Mrs. C. Temple Emmet, Sr., Christy (standing), *and brother William.*

The house itself, beside the many upstairs bedrooms, one of which was always assigned to me, had a music room, containing a grand piano and a harp. The piano had a pianola attachment and there was a great collection of rolls. There was also a huge phonograph, an early Victor with an enormous horn suspended above it. I also remember a table on which were magazines, mostly from Ireland and England. The dining room had a large table that revolved, so that you could serve yourself by spinning it around.

I soon learned that Chris had an enormous family, or so it seemed to me, an only child. Besides Chris, there were three sisters and two brothers. What interested me was that they all got along well. There was no fighting and they all loved one another. As a friend of Chris, the oldest brother, I was accepted as one of them. I was never treated as a guest, but as part of the family.

Mr. C. Temple Emmet, the head of the family, took a great interest in all his children and he would, from time to time, gather us together to read something to use he thought we ought to hear. This included, among other things, classics by Dickens and Scott. This would be mostly for the benefit of the younger members, but we would all listen. Like all his family, he had a beautiful voice. Mrs. C. Temple Emmet became like a second mother to me, because of my friendship with Christy. She was a devout Catholic, which the rest of the family were not, it seemed. She, too, had a great interest in all her children.

The conversations that took place were all of a cultural nature, about music and politics. I don't think I ever heard what we would call "gossip." It never entered their heads that anyone could be bad or evil in any way.

Christy and I played golf and tennis and attended many of the big tournaments, particularly those in Southampton and Forest Hills. Both Chris and his father were good squash players. They both enjoyed teaching me the fundamentals of what is now one of the most popular games in New York.

I became attached to another branch of the Emmet family, the Devereux Emmets, who lived nearby, and lived very much like the Temple Emmets. The head of the family, Devereux or Uncle Dev, as he was called, was one of the leading golf architects in the United States. The two sons, Richard and Devereux were great friends of Christy's and we all played together.

The living room in the Devereux Emmets' home had steps leading down to it, what we now call a "dropped" living room. One sort of made an entrance, and this so impressed me that I determined that should I ever build a house, it would have just such a room and, as it turned out, I later did.

There was one aspect of the Emmet family that meant little to me when I was growing up and that is its social background. When I got older, I realized that they were considered at the top of the social world. What this meant was that they belonged to the most important clubs that existed in New York at that time and that they were invited to the parties that constituted New York society. Even now, one hears in conversation reference to social backgrounds in such expressions as, "Who was she?" In Mrs. C. Temple Emmet's case, she was a Chanler, connected in some way or other with the Astors. Her name was Alida. I later learned that one of the granddaughters of the original John Jacob (The Great) Astor was named Alida. Another married into the Chanler family. There was never any discussion of working and possibly from these connections is where the money came from that kept the Emmet family going.

Being with Christy and his family opened up a new world for me. I was often not the only guest, for frequently a famous mu-

Christy Emmet in later life.

sician, artist or someone in the political arena would be there as well. One guest I remember was Pablo Casals, the cellist. I remember also coming into the living room one afternoon and sitting there at the piano was George Gershwin. This can be heady stuff for a young man.

In later life, Christy Emmet became the best known of all the Emmets. He was one of the first people here to recognize the danger of Hitler. After his death in 1974, in a tribute paid him it was said:

"Chistopher Emmet played a significant and at times important role in the development of the 20th Century American-German relations. One of the first Americans to sense the menace of Nazism in the early 1920's, he pioneered American opposition to it. By the time he died in 1974, his efforts, first in a purely private capacity, later as founder and guiding spirit of the American Council on Germany, had contributed substantially to the rebirth of war-torn West Germany, and to its transformation into a cornerstone of NATO and America's closest European ally."

The many honors Christy received were unknown to even his close friends, including me.

At any time, in any place, the Emmet family would have been extraordinary. I know my life was greatly enriched for knowing them.

MY FRIEND INGERSOLL

I called him "Ralph" and he called me "Bish." Two letters in the mail made me remember what he was like when we were young together at Yale and later in New York. The first letter was from Boston University to tell him that he would be given the degree of Doctor of Humane Letters at the commencement exercises, 1980:

"The degree is being awarded in recognition of your lifelong contributions to American newspaper and magazine journalism as an editor and publisher, for your books that have contributed materialy to the understanding of our culture and history, and as a public acknowledgement of your distinguished military carer."

The second letter, from Ralph Ingersoll, wished me a "Happy Birthday!" on my seventy-ninth. It is a letter I'll treasure. It said in part:

"Last night I had a dream featuring us both in our twenties. It was so vivid that I found myself turning on a light to convince myself that its inconsequential experience was not actually happening! That's how close I often feel to you—if that should be a comfort to you on your seventy-ninth birthday. In some strange way it was to me, to whom we are both still young squirts. So I wish you your Happy Birthday as one young squirt to an even younger!" (I am five months younger than he.)

Consulting Webster, I found that a "squirt" was "an insignificant, self-assertive fellow.'' Possibly, that definition did fit us both although, early on, I considered Ingersoll as having special talents.

We both had Irish nannies and supposedly played together as children in Central Park. I have no recollection of this, but it could be true. We do remember the soda fountain on 59th Street, run by a Miss Brennan. The ice cream soda, costing five to ten cents, was very popular in those days.

Our first real meeting was on Long Island, where we were both visiting the Emmet family and found that we were both going to Yale in the fall. Although, in many ways, we were different, we almost immediately became friends and remained so.

We had both been to different schools, Ingersoll to Kirmayer and Hotchkiss, and I to St. Bernard's and St. Paul's. Neither of us had any close friends going to Yale, and so we decided to room together. World War I prevented this happening until January of 1919.

From a physical standpoint, he was tall and thin, and not particularly coordinated. I played golf, squash and fenced. He preferred wrestling and probably would have played football, but he was studying engineering, which allowed little time for outside activities. (To this day, if the Yale team loses, he is close to tears.)

Ralph became an excellent student with seemingly little effort. He was often able to pick up some of the "ready" by writing papers for other students. He kept a diary and, from time to time, he would read to me from it; I think it was then that I became aware of his ability to write. I don't think he realized this himself, as it was not until many years later that he wrote his first book. While at Yale, he did not contribute to any of the literary organs, such as the Yale News or The Lit.

He loved to talk and, from our conversations, I learned something about his philosophy of life. Although he had grown up in a Christian family, I had the feeling that he questioned the common Christian beliefs. His ideas were more in tune with what we now call "interfaith." I had the honor of raising him to become a Master Mason, in later life.

He was a fighter for what he believed and never hesitated to get involved. I remember that one of our professors had got himself in some sort of trouble and Ralph, not only defended him, but went to the president of Yale to speak for him. His honorary degree speaks of his "military career" when, during World War II, Ralph was part of Dwight Eisenhower's team in London and took part in the invasion of Europe.

Even during our years at Yale, he was a great reporter. He

(Left) *Ralph McAllister Ingersoll at Yale and* (Right) *in the Army, World War II.*

could go to a party, a play, a game, and later describe in minute detail all that took place.

His father, who was a brilliant man, wanted Ralph to be an engineer like himself, and did not recognize until many years later, that his son was to be a great journalist.

As "young squirts," we both took an active part in the social life of New York. I became aware that Ralph McAllister Ingersoll had a social background through his family connection with Ward McAllister, who was responsbile for the so-called "400." For this reason, he was more in demand for parties than I was. I am not sure that he cared about society but, rather, it interested him as an observer of its rites and customs. Despite his seeming lack of coordination, he was a good dancer, particularly of the waltz, which I could never do. During this period, we both enjoyed being on the "stag line" and all the free food and entertainment that went with it.

Ralph was usually involved with a girl but, again, I think his interest was an attempt to understand our culture, rather than what we would consider "love," as generally defined.

From the Ritz ballroom his interest spread to the Pre-Catalan, one of New York's "spots" where the "bad girls" hung out. His interest in these girls was equally intense.

During my years in medical school, we saw less of each other. He had gone West and I had all I could do, keeping up with my studies. We kept up a correspondence, however, because we remained close friends after college.

It was when Ingersoll returned to New York that his genius as a writer and editor began to emerge. The New Yorker had just been established and he was hired to help run it and to write for it. It was a wonderful spot for him, for no one had a better knowledge and feel of the city than he, who had grown up in midtown.

He made a number of friends in the literary and artistic world of New York, including many members of the famous Algonquin Round Table. Because I was Ingersoll's friend, I was included in many parties. It was a great time to be young in New York.

This period of our friendship was soon to end, as our bachelor days would be over, and the life we led would not be the same again.

I do want to discuss how Ingersoll's friends reacted to PM, the unique newspaper venture which Ingersoll started and ran. When PM was started, Ralph and I were seeing a lot of each other and I heard much about it. The time was 1941, and I was just about to go into the Army. Ingersoll felt that he could be more valuable as a journalist, rather than enlisting. Later on, he was drafted and had a very illustrious career on Eisenhower's staff.

Many people were opposed to PM because they thought it was far to the left. The paper contained no advertising and Ingersoll felt this freed the editors from pressures from advertisers, so that they could write more freely. He was backed by monied friends who believed in him and in his ideas. The story of PM is very well told by E.J. Kahn in his recent book on John Hay Whitney, who was one of those backers.

My own personal reaction at that time was that he was my good friend and I wished him well in any venture he might undertake. I was busy with my own career and I was not in the literary world, so my interest was really as a bystander.

Ingersoll wrote very well himself and he had excellent people working for him. The publication failed, as everyone knows, but I think it is still rememberd as a unique venture in journalism.

Ingersoll and I, in those early days, rarely missed a Yale-Princeton or Yale-Harvard game. We always went together and this continued for many years. When the game was at Princeton, Ingersoll had the idea that we always ought to have breakfast at the Plaza. We would order an enormous breakfast, which would sort of lay a base for the drinking we would do at the game. It was always great fun. Up to now, I have missed very few Yale-Princeton games, and few Yale-Harvard games. The Yale Club would run a train or, later, a bus, but now that has all been given up.

There was one incident that occurred with Ingersoll, when we were young, just out of college. We went to a Yale-Harvard game in Boston. Coming back on the train, we got into a crap game. We did not each have a lot of money, so we pooled our resources. We got very, very lucky and, by the time the train got to New York, we had more or less cleaned out the other players, and as I recall, had winnings of about $500. As I think about it now, $500 in the twenties might be more like $1,000 today.

When we left the train, we decided to spend all the money as quickly as possible, just for the fun of it, because neither one of us had ever had $500 to spend as we wished.

The first place we went was to a speakeasy to have a few drinks, which we did not need at that point. We told the people at the bar about our good fortune, and they were so pleased with us and the game (Yale had won), that they would not allow us to pay for our drinks. When we left the speakeasy, our $500 was still intact.

We proceeded on to several nightclubs where we had modest checks, because the same thing happened. People kept picking up our tab and we had difficulty paying.

We finally wound up for the night in a Broadway hotel and, when we awoke the next morning, we had almost all the $500 we had won. It was curious that we, who, at that time, had so little money to spend, when we could, we couldn't!

Ingersoll and I often talked about it in later years.

So, thank you, "young squirt," for your friendship, through the good times and the bad times.

Chapter VII

Yale: World War I
and the Influenza Epidemic

THOSE "HAPPY, GOLDEN, BYGONE DAYS," about which we would later sing, were different from what we expected when we arrived at Yale in September, 1918. We were at war with Germany. Yale, as well as all other colleges, was operating on a wartime basis.

The Students Army Training Corps was on campus. S.A.T.C., as it was called, was part of the regular United States Army. It would prepare us for overseas duty. If you were eighteen or over, you would receive all the benefits as if you were in the regular Army. If you were under eighteen (I was seventeen), you were still under Army supervision. Yale was an armed camp.

Although we went to a few lectures, nearly all of our time was taken up learning to drill. We had to learn as much as possible about the Army in the shortest time. It was only because we lived on the Yale campus that we knew we were at Yale at all.

We lived under spartan conditions. We slept in a barracks and ate in a large dining room, similar to a "mess." We marched to our classes and were required to be in uniform at all times. We rose with the classic bugle call early in the morning and went to bed to "taps" at night.

The government had assigned a few officers from West Point to teach us the Army routine. We felt that they rather resented this assignment and made us as miserable as possible. We were neither students nor soldiers, but a combination of both. It was all very strange.

It was still possible to see the old fence where every Yale football captain had had his picture taken and in front of Connecticut Hall was the statue of Nathan Hale, a reminder that Yale was one of the oldest universities in the country. But there was no college life for us.

We had no time off, except Sundays. Each day was about sixteen hours in duration, all under Army supervision. What was curious was that we never fired a gun, but were required to do the manual of arms.

I have never been good with my hands and one difficulty I had was in putting on puttees. These are described in the dictionary as being "a long strip of cloth, wound spirally around the leg, from ankle to knee, worn by sportsmen, soldiers, etc." I never learned to do it correctly. They must be evenly wound or they look rather terrible and, in my case, they did.

I was assigned to the premedical company. As far as drilling was concerned, we were considered the worst on campus. In fact, we were so bad that, in short order, I found myself promoted from private to corporal!

My feeling during these months was that I was a tolerated volunteer, without a serial number, pay or indeed, any rights. We did know, though, that if the Army decided we were needed, we would be on our way overseas.

Then, early one morning, the bells from the many churches around the old campus began to ring out. We thought the war

Yale, World War I, Students Army Training Corps, September, 1918.

was ended, but we could not find out, because we were restricted to the barracks. It turned out to be a false alarm but, a few days later, came the real thing. Germany had surrendered and the war was over. A victory parade was ordered. We marched around New Haven for four hours, never breaking ranks.

We would remain a part of the Army for the next six weeks, then be formally discharged and allowed to go home for Christmas. Thus would end my "service" in World War I. I would not wear a uniform again until 1941.

Before we would go home, though, and just after the war ended, an influenza epidemic struck New Haven. Although army camps were struck with the disease in mid-September and, in fact, the whole country became involved, we in New Haven were spared until late fall.

As premedical students, most of us volunteered to work at New Haven Hospital. We had no real knowledge of medicine or nursing care, but felt we should try to be of help. The epidemic that I witnessed did not involve old and debilitated people, but nearly half the deaths were among men and women in their prime.

Even to a young prospective doctor, the clinical features of this disease were clear. The patient entered the hospital with what appeared to be a mild, febrile disease, which in a short time drastically worsened. The lungs filled with rales, the patients became short of breath and increasingly cyanotic. The color of the patients made a great impression on me and was described by clinicians of the time as a "violaceous heliotrope hue." This heliotrope cyanosis was sometimes confined only to the lips, earlobes and fingernails but, in severe cases, it was general over the face, trunk and extremities. The lips and mucous membranes were then often maroon and occasionally, the face and neck were lurid bluish-black, a discoloration neither attributed to circulatory failure nor related to the extent of the pneumonia.

Severe cases became delirious and incontinent, and died trying to clear their airways of the blood-tinged froth that gushed from the nose and mouth. It was dreadful to see.

It was reported, and it was true, that in our hospital about twenty percent of the total patient population died each night. There were not nearly enough doctors and nurses. Supplies were used up and undertakers ran out of coffins.

It was an exposure to medicine that I had not expected. I do not remember being afraid that anything might happen to me (all young people feel immortal) and, actually, none of us who helped contacted the disease. I do remember, though, feeling helpless because so little could be done. The disease then disappeared as suddenly as it had come.

I went home for Christmas, a soldier no more, and my hospital experiences provided the stimulus to go ahead with my premedical studies. After this unorthodox beginning, I looked forward to coming back to Yale after the New Year—to being a student again.

There was one other victory parade up Fifth Avenue in New York. I took part in it, along with others from S.A.T.C. Although we had done nothing for the war effort except drill on the New Haven campus, we got the same credit from the public as the returning veterans from Europe. History had recorded the terrible losses of our army during the last months of the War.

After the parade, my family took me to the Waldorf-Astoria Hotel, at that time on 34th Street and Fifth Avenue, where the Empire State Building stands today.

SHEFFIELD SCIENTIFIC SCHOOL

After Christmas vacation, I returned to New Haven to begin my education at Yale's Sheffield Scientific School. Here, a premedical course could be completed in three years. Graduating from this school almost guaranteed that you would be accepted into medical school. I lived in "Sheff Town" and no longer had any connection with the Old Campus or A.C. (Academic Campus), where the S.A.T.C. had been quartered.

Ralph Ingersoll and I had pledged that if we could, we would room together at Yale. We did just that all the time we were there and have remained lifelong friends.

Ralph had the same love for Yale that I did. He was born in New Haven. His father was a Yale graduate, which made Ralph a Yale "natural." He was five months older that I, and had also been through S.A.T.C., although I had not seen him during that time. He was an excellent scholar, planning now to study engineering.

The first school event was a torchlight parade of our class, called a "rush." For the first time, I experienced the Yale spirit, which would remain with me all my life.

A band played the Yale songs. Upper classmen, with a "Y" on their sweaters, took part and, suddenly, I wanted, more than anything else, acceptance as a "Yalie." In later life I have said, perhaps with just a touch of arrogance, that I never had to apologize for going to Yale.

When I am asked where to send a boy to college, I say that

Van-Sheff Towers.

it makes no difference where, but that the boy must identify with his school and appreciate its traditions if he is to benefit.

The next event of our class was the choosing of members for the various fraternities that were an important part of the school social system.

At Sheff, there were a number of fraternities at that time. Besides their Greek letters, they had other names. The best known were St. Anthony and St. Elmo. St. Anthony had the Greek letters $\Delta\ \Psi$ (Delta Psi) and St. Elmo, the Greek letters $\Delta\ \phi$ (Delta Phi).

My father had been a member of St. Elmo at Rutgers and Ralph's father a member of St. Anthony at Yale, so acceptance to these became very important to us.

Each fraternity was allowed to take fifteen men from our class. For about a week, you received many invitations to the various fraternities and selection was made on the final night.

Neither Ingersoll nor I were invited to join any of the Sheff societies. We felt socially banished. In a sense, it was like being "blackballed" in a club, in this case, a lot of clubs.

We soon found out, that many others had not been invited. This early experience did have an effect on me and, in later life, I think to compensate, I joined the "best" clubs to which I was eligible. Yet Yale meant a lot to me and I determined that I would be a credit to it, in one way or another. Athletics were in full swing and getting a "Y" in fencing became my goal. Fencing was considered a minor sport, but it was my best chance to get that "Y."

It was a blow to both of us when neither Ingersoll nor I were "tapped" for a fraternity. We were then presented with the problem of where to live. This was solved when we moved into 360 Temple Street, a small two-story house in New Haven, owned by the University. The house had an interesting history for, supposedly, Noah Webster had written his dictionary there. Years later, I heard that the house had been moved intact to a museum, not because we had lived there, but as part of an Americana exhibit.

Ingersoll and I moved into a large room on the second floor, which was to be our home for the next two years. With the others who lived there, we formed a congenial group and, in imitation of the fraternity system, we formed a club known as the "360," which came to have the same recognition as other organizations at Yale and subsequently found its way into the *Yale Banner and Potpourri* of 1920–21.

In a sense, "360" was a fraternity, because we lived together and played together. A lot of time was spent playing cards and shooting craps. Bridge was the card game of choice, but was not then played as it is now, where it is almost a science. There were several in my class thought to be supporting themselves playing bridge.

Our social life as a group also included dinners at New Haven's popular restaurants, such as the Hofbrau or the Bishop Hotel. We were supposed to eat our regular meals at what was called "Commons," but those of us who could afford it joined the Mory's Association (which I did) and would go there from time to time for dinner. When I was fencing, I was required to eat at the training table.

In retrospect, the main difference between us and the fraternity groups was that we had varied social backgrounds and were not all cut from the same mold. All of us did take part in Yale activities and several distinguished themselves on Yale teams. One thing was certain—we were all friends.

At Sheff and the academic side, there were other small groups of friends who went under such names as "Mohicans," "Mugwumps," "Potentates," "Tall Green Owls" and, of course, the world-famous "Whiffenpoofs," known for their singing. Only recently, I attended a dinner where the present-day Whiffenpoofs sang. There was a play in New York about them, called "Poor Little Lambs." It concerns a girl (Yale is now coed) who wants to be a "Whiff." The title is taken from the first line of the "Whiffenpoof Song": "We are poor little lambs who have lost their way. Bah. Bah. Bah."

SAVIN ROCK

At college there are always long sessions with a lot of talk. We called them "bull sessions." Today, it is called "rapping." I recently asked one of my old friends if he remembered what we talked about and he could not. His wife, who had attended a Western university, said that, at her school (as well as many others, probably), the topics were "boys," "sororities," "grades" and "future plans." At any rate, I think our informal conversations were as important to our growth as individuals as the formal education we received.

During our first spring at Yale we were introduced to a small amusement park called Savin Rock. There were a number of piers, shooting galleries, ferris wheels and a roller coaster. It had a certain charm, so when someone would say, "Let's go down to the Rock," it meant an evening of fun.

There were many restaurants there, where one could get a "shore dinner," which consisted of clam chowder, lobster or any kind of fish, corn on the cob, apple pie, ice cream and coffee. All this was usually washed down with beer and cost maybe $2. Very little hard liquor was consumed and cocktails were unknown.

My senior year, I also had a girl, Nan Moran, whom I took down there. I thought she was a beautiful girl. I can see her now. She was of Italian background and had dark hair. We used to sit having long talks, looking over the Sound. I can't say we were in love, but I was very fond of her. I was not her first Yale boy, she had been with others; but I was very attached.

I could not find out, even when I went back for my sixtieth reunion, whether or not Savin Rock still exists.

SEX EDUCATION

I was "on my own" as far as sex education was concerned. It was not taught in schools as it is today. It was not part of the family conversation. One might expect that, because my father was a doctor, he might have discussed the subject and given me advice, but I don't remember any discussion. My mother seemed to take it for granted that I would eventually learn what there was to know about it.

When I was at college and medical school and would stay out all night, no questions were asked. I would often just say that I would not be home, but would be staying with a friend.

At school, there were no girls except those who came up for special events, such as dances or at graduation time, so there was very little exposure there.

During vacation, there were many parties and dances, to which St. Paul's boys were invited, but the girls were chaperoned. One might steal a kiss on occasion, but that was all. The theatre and movies might contribute some further sex education, but pornography, as we know it today, did not exist.

So my sex education did not really begin until I became a freshman at Yale. In the bull sessions that took place at Yale, it was apparent to me that my friends knew more about it than I did, or possibly they pretended to. So, at Yale, I began to explore this new world and my friend Ingersoll was a good companion for this project. I became aware that certain types of girls "turned me on," as they say these days. One of these was the movie queen, Norma Talmadge.

In New York, in this period, the early 20's, there were a number of rather wild parties called "balls." One of these was the Fakers Ball, which Ralph and I attended. There seemed to be a good deal of sex connected with them, but not as far as we were concerned. Many boys from the Ivy League schools attended these balls and there would be much conversation about them.

In reading my diary of that period, I noted an entry dated April 4, 1919, saying that my good friend Christy Emmet and I had gone to the PreCat. This institution contributed to the sex education of much of the Ivy League, particularly Yale and Princeton. Harvard never seemed in evidence and no doubt had another haunt.

The PreCat was originally an old New York restaurant called Bustanobys (there was a joke about it that it could bust anybody). It then became a night club with a small floor show. Its principal attraction was that you could pick up a girl there and take her home. A regular group of girls went there every night to be picked up. They were not prostitutes, but had particular friends they enjoyed being with. Of course, their check would be paid. To this day I remember some of their names: there was Helen Smith, a fat girl with a beautiful face; May Dorsey, who was a great favorite with the Princeton boys; and a girl named Trixy, whom I particularly liked.

In Europe, it was the custom for a father to take his son to a girl whom he knew and trusted to instruct his son in the facts of life. At the PreCat, we virgins were on our own and, in my case, it fell to Trixy to do the honors. There was no exchange of money—she was simply a friend who liked you and to whom you might or might not give a present. Of course, this type of institution no longer exists. I am sorry that the PreCat was not given landmark status for I think, for its contributions to the education of the many who went there, it deserved that honor more than many landmarks around today.

The New York singles bars may function somewhat in the same way and I have heard that certain bars cater to various groups, including one or two on the Upper East Side where preppy types can be found.

There were available girls in New Haven with whom one could indulge in "necking," this being further broken down into "light" or "heavy." One problem encountered would be that these girls were not accustomed to drinking and would suddenly get sick, which brought the evening to an abrupt end.

In my diary of 1919 (I was eighteen years old), I note in back, "Leonie Cauchois, 111 Osborn Place, Kew Gardens, Richmond Hill 5040." She was my first experience with what it meant to "have a crush." To me it meant that, despite contact with other girls at dances and parties, one girl absorbed my thoughts and was never out of my mind. I was often afraid even to touch her. For the first time I felt that deep emotion, jealousy. A young man will take these feelings very seriously, sometimes to a point where it can have a very bad effect. In my own case, there could be no thought of marriage, as I was still in college. Today, with the so-called sexual revolution, things are different. Young people caring for each other live together, even in college.

In all events, returning to school cooled the relationship, although there remained a lingering feeling of what might have been for some time. And then, it was over. During the growing up period, I think this occurred many times.

A further step in my sex understanding occurred in my senior year in college when, for the first time, I would spend several days at a time with a girl. In New Haven, there were a number of inns where one could do this. You were assigned a cabin attached to the roadhouse, which insured total privacy. Girls who did this did not confine themselves to a relationship with one man although in some instances, as in my own case, a close relationship can evolve.

This was the first time I became aware of what total exposure to a woman meant. There were little things to illustrate this. I had never had the experience of going to bed and waking up with a girl alongside me. I had no idea that she would cook breakfast and enjoy being with me after our sex relationship was over. I knew that girls had similar body functions, but had never been around when they took place. I'm sure that I was not unique and that spending time with a girl was part of the learning process of all young men.

The last step in sex education is when there is sex with a friend with no intention of marriage. She may be seeing other men, and you, other girls.

During my medical school days in New York, there were many girls who worked and had their own apartments. They were often glad to have a friend and sex partner. You would invite her to dinner, possibly a show, and on occasion, bring her a present.

Years later, I remember a friend, discussing these relationships, who said: "I can't afford it. I can pay a hooker, but when it's free, it becomes very expensive. This kind of girl is always behind in the rent."

I did not feel that way and I had at least one very good relationship of this kind. We never forgot one another and, not too long ago (sixty years later), she called me on the telephone, because she had seen my name in a book one of my patients had written. It was sweet to talk to her again, but I had the feeling we would not have wanted to meet. "You can't go home again."

RIOT

In the spring of my freshman year at Yale, a most dramatic thing happened and that was a full-scale riot. I had not realized there was bad feeling between the townspeople of New Haven and Yale University, but apparently this had always been so. "Town and gown" is a classic animosity. Underlying this animosity was the feeling that for the most part, at that time, Yale students were considered part of the privileged social class and this was resented in town.

This confrontation was a particularly bad one, as many young men had just returned from the war, both in New Haven and at Yale, and there was a general feeling of unrest. Supposedly the reason for the riot was that Yale students who were war veterans had refused to march in an American Legion Parade. This was not entirely true, as some of the S.A.T.C. did take part, but most of the Yale veterans refused.

The first we heard of the fighting was that some boys from Yale had been attacked by boys from New Haven. It is possible to lock up the students on campus by closing the gates, but this was not possible in Shefftown, where we were.

The riot lasted nearly three days, and a lot of students as well as "townies" were hurt, including innocent bystanders. The police had little impact, and it seemed to me that it gradually quieted down as the parties wearied.

When you are young, as we were, you are caught up in the excitement, but in later years, I realized what a terrible thing it was, and how it can happen at any time, for little reason.

Yet, in the future, many of Yale's heroes would come from New Haven, such as the great Levi Jackson, a black, born in New Haven, who would, in the 1940's, become Yale's football captain. He was only one of many town boys to go to Yale.

FENCING

The first thing I learned that freshman year was how difficult a premedical course really is. It requires a lot of study, which cuts down the time for other things you might want to do. Physics, mathematics, biology and German were the subjects that gave me the most difficulty. I also found the college professors quite different from the previous schoolmasters I had known, in that they usually gave you a "break" if they felt you were trying. Yale also offered opportunities for special tutoring before exams, which included special sessions conducted by my old school, Rosenbaum's.

Sheffield Scientific School, because the course was completed in three years, had a more weighted schedule than did the academic side of Yale. Although we did not know it, we were to be the last three-year class. This accelerated course did mean a lot of studying but, with it all, I did manage to do other things. There is no question in my mind that this does make for a more well-rounded education.

Although fencing was to be my one athletic achievement at Yale, I took a shot at wrestling, and although I was not very good, I found it a good tough conditioning sport. I developed a boil on my arm, and had to stop wrestling. I often wonder why I tried it at all.

University Fencing Team 1921. (Top row, left to right) *Senac (Ch.), Davenport, Plumley and Hanway.* (Bottom) *Bishop, Walker and MacKenzie.*

My father had given me fencing lessons in New York, which was a good start into the fencing world at Yale. It is helpful when an older student takes an interest in you, and such was the case with me. The best fencer was a boy named Lester. He was a superb athlete and won the Intercollegiate title the following year. He encouraged me in every way and told me that, if I would work at it, I could not only fence on the team, but he wanted me to try out for Assistant Manager, because that way I could manage the team in my senior year.

As one of the freshman team, I took part in a few meets. This was the first time I realized what it means to train as an athlete.

Fencing, although a minor sport with a small squad compared to other sports such as swimming, basketball and hockey, had a definite training period of its own.

To be a good fencer requires long hours of practice and expert coaching. It is necessary to train a special set of muscles and to have very precise coordination, as much depends on quick reflex movements.

My own personal contribution to the Yale fencing team was to fence foil, one of the three weapons used in intercollegiate events. The other two are sabre and epee. The foil team consisted of three men. The number one man was A.P. Walter, Jr. who was captain. I was number two, and L.I. MacKenzie was number three.

All the athletes involved in minor sports were required to eat at the training table, where a special diet was served, geared to the athlete. Being required to do this made you feel good, because although you played a minor sport, you were a part of a Yale team, and taken no less seriously than if you played Yale football.

In the gym, next to the fencing room, the swimming team trained before being allowed into the tank. Their coach and trainer was Bob Kiphuth, who proved to be the greatest swimming coach of all time.

I want to skip ahead again here, to my senior year at Yale. I did pretty well in fencing as an individual, and the team only lost to the Navy, which was a good record. I had a lot of satisfaction in the Harvard meet, where I had lost the year before, when I beat an old rival of mine who was also one of my good friends, Samuel Ordway.

As manager of the fencing team, I accepted an invitation to go down to Bridgeport with the team to have a meet with the Bridgeport team. It seemed strange that fencing, which at that time was recognized as a sport only in the big schools and in a few large athletic clubs, should even exist in Bridgeport. We went and it was soon evident why we had been invited. There was a young man there, a Belgian, named Robert Grasson, who was not only a great athlete, but one of the most attractive and dynamic personalities that I would ever meet. We won that meet from the Bridgeport team, but only because we had more experience.

I have often wondered what led me as manager of the team to accept that rather unusual invitation to Bridgeport. It could only have been to meet Grasson, if one believes in fate.

The following year, Bobby Grasson came to Yale as fencing

coach, and put the team on top for many years to come. I never had the satisfaction of having Grasson as coach and only knew him through our meets with Bridgeport. I had the feeling that he would become one of the all-time greats in this sport and that is what happened.

I thought that I might be able to get some more recollections of Bobby Grasson from C.M. DeLand, Jr. (Yale, '22), who won the intercollegiate epee championship in my senior year and who lives near me now in the country. Unfortunately, all he could tell me was that Grasson began his coaching career in 1922. This again emphasized to me the advantage of keeping a diary. There must be millions of diaries and I heard recently of a place where they can be deposited for future historians to use.

When Bobby Grasson died, he was so beloved by the Yale fencing fraternity that a fund was established to care for his widow.

Besides being part of the Yale team, I would come down to New York from time to time to take part in fencing events. I won one of these, which gave me a lot of publicity as a good junior fencer and a possible candidate for the Olympic team. The meet was called the Hammond Foils. I don't know if it still exists, but it was important at that time. In the intercollegiates, which wind up the season in New York, and is, in a sense, the climax of the year, I did very badly, for no reason I could explain.

It is traditional at Yale, as no doubt elsewhere, to have a banquet at the end of the season, where there are speeches and toasts. In addition, all Yale teams are photographed as a permanent record and the pictures later appear in the *Yale Banner* and *Potpourri*.

This was the 1920-21 season. After the fencing season ended at Yale, my interest in sports shifted to racquet games, which became an important part of my life. I had always been very interested in tennis, so when the competition to become manager began, I applied. Again, I was anxious to do something to insure myself a "letter." The manager of a team is awarded a minor sport "Y," the same the team receives. But there is a lot of work involved and, after a period of time, I had to drop out.

MUSIC AND THEATRE

My junior year at Yale was difficult, as I tried to resolve the conflict between my studies and my outside activities. I had taken a premedical course, which was very difficult, and my studies included organic chemistry, physics, psychology, comparative anatomy and others equally demanding. On the other hand, I had a real interest in the university, and wanted to be part of its activities, social and otherwise. I now think that what one really gets out of attending a university is that one is exposed to the best of everything. This is true at other universities as it was true at Yale.

The finest performers appeared at concerts in New Haven and I remember hearing the violinist, Jascha Heifetz, and thinking at the time that I would like to learn to play the violin. What was important was that most of us could afford tickets to these concerts, which nearly always were sold out.

I continued to try many things, which were not always successful. I had had a few mandolin lessons at school, and a few more on vacation, and I thought I played well enough for the Mandolin Club, which was a relatively important organization at that time. One could say the mandolin enjoyed the same vogue then as the guitar does today. At the mandolin trials, I played very badly and was told there was no place for me. Surprisingly, there were many good players at Yale.

I had always thought that I could act and even considered acting as a career. I tried out for the Yale Dramat. I was considered, but finally was told that I was not accepted. Two of my friends, who presented a short play with me in the tryouts, did succeed and were elected.

Later, I did appear as an extra in a mob scene in "Tamburlaine." It was performed at the Yale Bowl. All of the performers received a Drama watch charm for their efforts, but important for me was the fun of being in a production. Acting was one of the things I most enjoyed doing.

It was also during my junior year that I tried to become part of the outside community life at New Haven and worked in some of the boys clubs. I coached a cast of youngsters and actually produced a play. I cannot remember its title or whether it had any merit but it seemed successful and gave me a great deal of personal satisfaction. I think this went back to my interest and training at St. Bernard's.

At that time, New Haven did offer the theatre experience to anyone interested, as many New York productions tried out at the Shubert before opening in New York. One of my greatest friends, Roland (Poly) Hooker, loved the theatre as I did and we rarely missed any play that came along. I think that the greatest one we ever saw was "John Ferguson." This was written by St. John Ervine. It was a tragedy set in Ireland and portrayed a simple farmer who had exalted standards of conscience. It was an instant success and, when it opened in New York with Dudley Digges as the star, it supposedly rescued the Threatre Guild from bankruptcy. The play was beautifully acted and made a deep impression on Roland and me.

After an evening at the theatre, we usually went on to Mory's. To this day, it is my philosophy and enjoyment to go to the theatre and then on to supper to eat and discuss the play. I think dining before is a great mistake.

TRADITIONS

At this time, I think it is impossible to take a premedical course at college and to do anything else, because the requirements for entrance to medical school are so high, requiring an A or B+ average. This was not the case in my day. My average was in the C+ range throughout my Yale days. I constantly worried about "flunking out" but would not give up my other interests. I think I wanted to enjoy my Yale experience to the fullest—to be a part of a great university.

In re-reading Scott Fitzgerald's *This Side of Paradise,* I can identify with his main character, Amory (whom I assume is Fitzgerald):

> He liked knowing that Gothic architecture, with its upward trend that was peculiarly appropriate to universities, and the idea became personal to him. The silent stretches of green, the quiet halls with an occasional late burning scholastic light held his imagination in a strong grasp, and the chastity of the spire became a symbol of this perception.

I had this same feeling about Yale and, although we lived some distance from much of the Gothic architecture, it was always there. Again, I felt this way when, in later life, I visited Oxford and Cambridge.

Why Yale? My father would have liked me to go to Rutgers where he had become a trustee, but, for me, my first choice was Yale and my love for this school would remain throughout my life.

As I have said, over the years, I have attended almost every Yale-Princeton and Yale-Harvard football game. Bob Cooke, a friend of mine in later years, had a job broadcasting Ivy League games and, on one occasion, during a Yale-Princeton game in the Yale Bowl, he described the sky as blue, and then he added,

"Yale blue." Yale had just completed a pass to the Princeton three-yard line. He then added, "I know my friend, Doctor Bishop is listening in," (I was, having missed going) "and would have enjoyed seeing this."

Cooke was so biased toward Yale that I later heard, although I am not sure it is true, that these remarks cost him his Ivy League broadcasting career.

My special feeling about Yale never changes. Perhaps it is that "Yale blue" to which Bob Cooke refers, or the bulldog, the Yale symbol, or those wonderful songs: "At a table down at Mory's, at a place where Louis dwells . . ." and ending, "We are poor little lambs, who have lost their way. Baa, baa, baa"; or, "March on Down the Field," the inspiring football song written by Cole Porter; or, "The Undertaker Song," a sort of mournful dirge, sung only at Yale-Princeton or Yale-Harvard games when the game is "on ice" for Yale. It is a mournful dirge, yet filled with ill-concealed joy, and accompanied by the waving of white handkerchiefs from the Yale stands:

> *More work for the undertaker*
> *Another little job for the casket maker*
> *In the local cemetery they are very very busy*
> *on a brand new grave.*
> *No hope for Harvard.*

Whenever I attended a game, I stayed from the kickoff until the last whistle blew. I never left until I heard:

> *In after years, should troubles rise*
> *To cloud the blue of sunny skies*
> *How bright will seem through memories haze*
> *Those happy golden bygone days.*
> *Then let us strive that ever we*
> *May let those words our watch-cry be*
> *Where upon life's sea we sail*
> *For God, for country, and for Yale.*

GRADUATIONS

Every spring there is a ritual enacted in colleges throughout our land called "graduation." I have attended three Yale graduations: my own (1921), my son's (1956) and my grandson's (1978).

In most cases, the families of the graduating students appear. It has often been a real sacrifice to put the student through school. In my own instance, this was not so, but I had the feeling, nevertheless, that my parents were proud to see me graduate.

There were certain circumstances surrounding my graduation of which they were not aware or, if they were, they were discreet enough not to mention. I had spent the two days before graduation with a girl at the nearby Rustic Inn and almost did not get back in time for the graduation.

EPILOGUE

In May, 1981, I returned with my wife for the sixtieth class reunion at Yale of '21 Sheff. When the bus brought us to our headquarters, someone asked, "What class is this?"

The answer was, " '21 Sheff, or what's left of it!" This was not entirely true. Our original class numbered 400. Ninety are said to be alive. Seventeen returned, some with wives, either first or second. At sixty years out, some were physically not up to coming and some, perhaps, financially, as it is not an inexpensive three-day outing.

60th Class Reunion, '21 Sheff. Yale.

The sixtieth is considered the next to the last reunion to take place. Most men will be in their late eighties at the sixty-fifth. I saw a few of the class of '16 Sheff. There were only five and it seemed to me that it must have been a great effort for them to be there.

Greeting one's classmates is made easy by virtue of a large name badge. My old friends were not there. My closest friend, Ingersoll, did not come. Sadly, many of my other friends were dead. The faces of those at the reunion looked familiar, but seemed like shadows out of the past.

Ours was a typical reunion with luncheons and banquets, including our class dinner at the most famous of Yale restaurants, Mory's, which was unchanged and still remains a landmark. All the festivities were preceded by rather moderate drinking. I observed we did not overindulge. Some did not drink at all. I also noted that there was no smoking, except for one pipe. Conversation consisted in a certain amount of reminiscence, but there was a good deal of discussion about successes in various directions.

There were two other doctors there who had taken the premedical course with me. One had been a great financial success, had built a hospital and had a son who was a neurologist. The other was an orthopedic surgeon, although this was overshadowed by his success as a tennis player. He has played all over the world and even played some tennis during our weekend. He seemed the most vigorous of all the classmates and, psychiatrically, even at this late age, he appeared hypomanic.

I did talk with some of the others and one, in particular, seemed to me to have had a happy life. He was from Minneapolis, successful in retail ladies wear (a far cry from our scientific courses), married 55 years, with children and grandchildren. He seemed a contented man.

We were invited for cocktails to the home of one of our classmates, who lived nearby, and then to the Pine Orchard Country Club for lunch, a familiar place to returning classes.

One morning, fairly early, I decided to take a walk alone, purely for a little nostalgia of my own. I intended to visit the Yale Art Museum, but it was closed. This involved walking on Chapel Street, which brought back many memories. This was a street where, when we were students, we would pick up girls. Closing my eyes, I remembered how young and pretty they were. I thought back to the girl I had known who nearly caused me to miss graduation. The thought came to me that they were old ladies now, and I wondered if they ever think of those days, "those happy, golden, bygone days."

Suddenly, there was the old Taft Hotel, which was still standing, but was either being renovated or torn down. I could not go in because of the construction, but I would have liked to see the bar, where I had my first cocktail. It was called a "Jack Rose," unknown to bartenders of the present day. I would have liked to see the lobby, too, where we used to meet before football games.

The Shubert Theatre used to be next to the Taft, but no longer is there. This was a theatre I loved as an undergraduate, as here we saw many shows in out-of-town tryouts. I thought of some of the great performances I had seen there. "John Ferguson" was one.

As I continued up Chapel Street, I remembered the Smoke Shop, where we used to bet on games, but I could not find it. I then wandered over to the New Haven green and sat a while. There were some friendly pigeons. The green seemed larger than I remembered it, when you could cross it in a few minutes. There are several churches on the green, and I stopped in for a minute at Old Trinity, which was built in 1752. It was empty, except for a young man cleaning.

I then walked back and into the old Yale campus, where we had lived and drilled in 1918, before World War I ended. The old campus is beautiful in the sunlight, and has changed least of all. There is still the statue of Nathan Hale in front of Connecticut Hall, where his room was situated.

My nostalgic walk over, I returned to the new, shiny hotel, the Park Sheraton, to join my classmates for lunch.

Chapter VIII

European Trip

AN AMERICAN CUSTOM WHICH STILL EXISTS, perhaps in a somewhat different form than in the early twenties, was, if you could afford it, to give your son a trip to Europe after graduation from college, either a formal tour or just to have him go by himself or with a friend. The idea was that, after this experience, he would come back to some sort of business or, in other cases, start his professional study, either in law or medical school. In my own case, I would be returning to medical school.

In all events, I was taken to Europe by my family, and then was to be allowed to go on my own to Rome from England. Fortunately, I would join some of my good friends, so that I would not be completely alone.

It is an advantage to a young man to be exposed to Europe at an early age, if it is possible. Many men who later gained prominence had this experience. I recently worked on some lectures about Washington Irving, who went to Europe at an early age and absorbed many interesting things. He kept an accurate diary. The trip was called "The Grand Tour," which was perceived as visiting London, Paris and Rome. I kept my own diary, much of which is drawn upon in this chapter, about the things I saw and my reaction to them as a young man.

I was fortunate in having a family who considered travel important. Being an only son, I went everywhere my parents went and I also spent time traveling with my friends.

I had been to Europe before, but was too young at the time to fully appreciate what Europe had to offer. In 1921, Europe was only reached by boat. My family preferred the English lines and so, as a result, we sailed on what was then called the White Star Line. The boat was the S.S. Cedric. Crossing the ocean by boat is a thing of the past, but looking back on it, it was great fun.

There were a number of young men aboard from various schools. We did much eating and talking. Bridge was becoming very popular and we played a lot. The trip was a smooth one. I think one of the most dramatic travel experiences is seeing land after one has traveled by boat across the ocean. This is something that the air traveler misses. In our case, we saw the lights of Liverpool.

LONDON

My first exposure to London was the beginning of a love affair with that city that has endured to this day.

The first thing most people do when coming to a new city is to walk around. This I did and would do many times on future trips but I never lost my feeling of discovery. Before leaving me to explore London on my own, my family took me to see the Cheshire Cheese, where Ben Johnson presided, and to Simpson's, which at that time was the place for roast beef.

I was to learn that London was a place where a man could get the proper clothes. My father, on arriving, immediately went round and ordered some suits and shirts for himself and this was a forecast of what I would do myself later in life whenever I went to London, although the next time would be some thirty years off. There is no place on earth where as much attention is paid to a man's appearance and it is rare to see an Englishman badly dressed on any occasion. The English tailor is a legend, even up to the present time. At that early age, my father stressed to me the importance of being well-dressed in your daily contacts. He would say, "If you have something important to do, dress up to the occasion." I have tried to do this.

I might say that, after wearing clothes "made-to-order," clothes "off-the-rack" do not feel quite the same, although they come at a much lower cost. For some reason, shirts made in England have not been duplicated in this country. In England, the shirtmaker occupies a position equal to the English tailor.

Even my first cup of tea was a new experience. Why is this so? There is no doubt it is different. During my later medical life, I took care of an elderly and rather well-to-do lady who sent to London for her tea *and* for the *water* for her tea, so that it would be just as she liked it. She didn't think the water in the U.S. was any good. Perhaps it has to do with the whole ritual of tea, which is so much a part of the English way of life, even their philosophy, just as it is in Japan.

Then came my first experience with the London theatre. The first show I was taken to see was one of the great plays of the twenties, "The Circle" by Somerset Maugham. It was considered a shocking comedy. It was said about "The Circle," "The characters had more poise and sinned with the elegance of people bred to vice and ease." Somerset Maugham introduced a new type of comedy which was very popular at this time. John Drew would eventually star in this play in New York with Mrs. Leslie Carter.

The theatre was a nightly event. We saw "If," by the playwright, Lord Dunsany, and "A Bill of Divorcement," by Clemence Dane. I loved this play, which later made a star of Katherine Cornell, who was described by Heywood Broun as "an American Duse."

In addition, London always had a great melodrama and at that time it was "Out to Win." This form of theatre is not around anymore. By definition (Webster's) "melodrama" is "a variety of drama, commonly romantic and sensational with both song and instrumental music interspersed; hence any romantic and sensational drama, typically with a happy ending."

What makes the London theatre the finest in the world? There are many opinions about this. Even at my early age, there were things I became aware of regarding this, which have not been changed up to the present time. For one thing, the theatre performance started early, so that one had supper afterwards. That has been tried in New York, and without success. I do think the only way to really enjoy a play is with a clear head and an empty stomach. Afterwards, one can enjoy supper leisurely and discuss the entertainment. Theatre tickets were cheap and easy to obtain, except for the big hits. Then too, the quality of the acting was nearly always exceptional. I think it was the great English actor, David Garrick, who said, "There are no small parts." Although there were great stars on the London stage, there was no "star system." Today, when I invite someone to go the theatre, the first question they are apt to ask is, "Who is in it?" A practical point about the London theatres is that they are easier to get in and out of. Tea and coffee were served between the acts, and a bar was available. All of these amenities made theatre-going a delightful experience. New York has copied these things to some extent, but it has taken a long time.

On this trip, I was taken to an English music hall, the most famous being the Palladium, the equivalent of the old Palace in New York. The most famous entertainers in England appeared here, accompanied by lesser acts. There was always an animal act and a magician, in addition to the usual singers and dancers. Later I heard about the Bing Boys, who played during World War I, and were well-known to English and American troops.

Because of my fencing at Yale and the possibility that I might be Olympic material, my father encouraged me to fence in the mornings, at what was the leading fencing academy in London, called Bertrand's. Fencing is taken more seriously in Europe than in the U. S. and, at the time, I was impressed with the quality, particularly, of the women who trained there.

We also went to see the sights of London because, according to plan, I was to take off to the continent almost immediately. My family picked out two essential places I must see. One was Westminster Abbey and the other was the British Museum. I now know that the British Museum cannot be covered in less than a week, but no one can visit Westminster Abbey even briefly without realizing what a part it has played in English history. I was deeply impressed with the Abbey and later would visit it whenever I was in London.

Dr. Samuel Johnson said, "When a man is tired of London, he is tired of life, for there is in London all that life can afford." A line from Alexander Pope is equally appropriate, "Dear, damned, distracting town." Only recently I heard another quotation from Marshal Blucher, the Prussian who helped defeat Napolean at Waterloo. Gazing at London for the first time from St. Pauls, after the great victory, Blucher muttered gruffly, "*Was für plünder*! What loot!" Hitler must have thought the same thing when, many years later, the Battle of Britain was fought.

My first exposure to London and England was really a great experience and has impressed on me the importance of travel in one's education. Experiencing, seeing, hearing the great and the lesser wonders of our time will greatly enrich your life. Often one must travel to do this.

PARIS

My trip to Paris was by train all night in a sleeper, which arrived at six o'clock in the morning. I have no recollection of the trip except, for the first time, I was on my own in Europe with enough money in a letter of credit to carry me for awhile. I had the feeling my family was somewhat anxious about my traveling alone, but this is no doubt true of all families.

On arrival in Paris, I met my friends, Ingersoll and Hooker, my college roommates. They were on their way that day to Rome. They had chartered an aeroplane and pilot to fly them there, which was unheard of in the twenties. The reason for doing it was that Hooker had met a girl on the boat going over and had decided he wanted to marry her. Ingersoll was to help him win her over. Hooker was rich and could afford to hire an aeroplane.

They persuaded me to follow them there the next day, which meant another long train trip, and so I only had one day and one night to catch my first glimpse of Paris.

At the time, as a young inexperienced boy, I could not really appreciate the meaning of Paris. I was disappointed not to be with my friends. I did not realize I was in a city during a period that would be later immortalized, for at that time it was a haven for some of the greatest literary and artistic talents of all time, such people as Ernest Hemingway, Scott Fitzgerald, James Joyce, Pablo Picasso, Igor Stravinsky and Serge Diaghilev. But I saw the Louvre and the Eiffel Tower. Many years later, when we visited Paris with my daughter, she would refer to it as the "Awful Eiffel."

That summer of 1921, incredible as it may sound, a dollar would get you sixteen francs and even more if you were willing to deal in the black market.

In later life, I had the opportunity to visit one of the best-known clubs in Paris, The Travellers, but, at that time, the only club I had heard of was Harry's Bar, and this is where every American college boy would find himself at five o'clock in the afternoon, hopefully awaiting the beginning of a big evening. Meeting someone there from the States was always an excuse for a celebration.

The main interest was the night life of Paris, which could not be duplicated in any city in the world. For the first time, I also saw the outdoor cafe, where one could linger with a coffee or a drink for an indefinite time. The most popular cafe was the Café de la Paix. Such cafes have become part of the New York scene only over the past few years.

That night I devoted to exploring the night life of the Montmartre, including a visit to the Folies Bergères, a place that takes in more tourist dollars than any other theatre. At the time, the Folies was considered daring, because of the statuesque nudes who were not permitted to move. Today, we would consider this rather corny. As far as the costumes and scenery were concerned, it seemed to me the Ziegfield Follies in New York was far more sumptuous.

I ended up that evening at the famous restaurant, Ciro's, which I believe still exists. There I met up with or, more correctly, picked up a Russian girl named Sonia. I would have liked to visit the famous "spots" of Paris (at that time, the boys

The Travellers' Club.

talked about "The House of All Nations") but there was not time nor money.

Even this short exposure to Paris was worthwhile because, as time went by, I began to appreciate the little I had seen. World War I had not been over very long. Alan Seeger, one of the young poets of the era, was killed charging up to the German trenches. He wrote a poem about Paris, which in my opinion, says it all. The first verse is:

> *First London, for its myriads, for its height,*
> *Manhattan heaped in towering stalagmite*
> *But Paris for the smoothness of the paths*
> *That lead the heart unto the heart's delight.*

Then he goes on to what I was at twenty, as were others, but surely did not appreciate it:

> *Fair loiterer on the threshold of those days*
> *When there's no lovelier prize the world displays*
> *Than having beauty and your twenty years*
> *You have the means to conquer and the ways.*

And finally at the end of his beautiful poem, he sums up his reaction to the city with these final verses:

> *And when all else is gray and void in the vast*
> *gulf of memory,*
> *Green islands of delight shall be all blessed*
> *moments so enjoyed,*
> *When vaulted with the city skies on its cathedral*
> *floors you stood*
> *And priest of a bright brotherhood performed*
> *the*
> *mystic sacrifice*
> *At love's high altar fit to stand with fire and*
> *incense aureoled*
> *The celibrant in cloth of gold with spring and*
> *youth in either hand.*

ROME

At that time there was a direct train from Paris to Rome. I think it was simply the Rome-Paris Express. It left Paris at 11:40 a.m.

and arrived in Rome the next day. Like most European trains, it was very comfortable. The food, the lovely French and Italian scenery, the interesting travelling companions you met, all made it a fine trip. We stopped at Menton, the town at the border between France and Italy, and there was much excitement as there was a crew change and all that goes with entering another country. After this, I finally got to bed, and arrived in Rome rather tired and worn out.

I met my friends at the Excelsior Hotel, one of the grand hotels of Europe then and now. I remember the marble floors and I remember quite clearly the first lunch, consisting first of the most delicious antipasto.

The plan I had was to spend a week in Rome with my two friends from Yale, and later we would be joined by a third Yalie. Our immediate problem was to help Hooker, who wanted to marry the girl he had met on the boat, and who was our main reason for being in Rome.

The girl's name was Betty and she turned out to be a beautiful blonde, who was scheduled to appear in a film her uncle was producing, called, interestingly enough, "The Fall of Rome." I do not remember ever seeing the finished picture, but I was told she was to play one of the slave girls.

The Italian marriage laws are very complicated for Americans and it was finally decided they would have to wait until they got back. Betty Hooker and I later became good friends, after she and Poly married, and we remained so for the next fifty years, until she died a few years ago.

Between our various conferences about the marriage, we did manage to do some sightseeing, and there was much to see. Rome has been described as a city which commanded the greatest Empire the world has ever known, where Jews and Christians were once the same, and which brought the lifeblood of Greece to the world, as well as its own.

A guidebook convinced me that if I stayed in Rome for a year, I would still not see everything. The whole city is a museum. Later, in 1960, when I returned for the Olympic Games, I was to continue my sightseeing. We did, however, do things that first time that left a lasting impression. We saw St. Peter's by moonlight and we walked through the Villa Borghese. We also spent a whole day at the Vatican. It is only recently that I realized that the Vatican is a capital, not merely of Roman Catholicism, but, symbolically, of Christianity itself.

It is probably not there now, but I remember we went to a

restaurant on a hill overlooking Rome. It was called the Castello de Cesari. We also took a few trips outside Rome to Tivoli and "the Villa d'Este, one of the prettiest places on earth," so recorded in my diary.

We only spent a week in Rome, but it was very special. After I took my daughter around the world, she wrote me, "I may return to some of the places we went, but it will never be as exciting as the 'first time.' " I know I felt the same way about Rome.

I also remembered Thomas Macaulay's poem, "Horatius," from "Lays of Ancient Rome," which I had learned at St. Bernard's School. I thought of it when I saw the ancient Tiber River for the first time:

> Lars Porsena of Clusium
> By the Nine Gods he swore
> That the great house of Tarquin
> Should suffer wrong no
> more.
> By the Nine Gods he swore it,
> And named a trysting day,
> And bade his messengers ride
> forth
> East and west and south and north
> To summon his array . . .
>
> Oh, Tiber! father Tiber!
> To whom the Romans pray,
> A Roman's life, a Roman's arms,
> Take thou in charge this day.

FLORENCE

One of my Yale friends, Allen Cooper Diefendorf, known at Yale as Diefy, who had had a distinguished athletic career, accompanied me on the rest of the trip through Italy. We planned to spend one day in Florence and then continue on to Venice. We had no real knowledge of art, but nevertheless we darted around the various galleries. Finally, I saw something that rang a bell. Outside the wall of a hospital, were the della Robbia babies. They have that lovely blue color. There was a copy of one of them in our bathroom at home. Since then, I have learned that everyone knows about them who is interested in Florentine art.

It was a quick look at a city I was never to visit again. My son-in-law took his family there this summer, and of course, they saw the della Robbia babies.

VENICE

Later Diefy and I took the night train to Venice, arriving there in the morning. We were young, and did not appreciate that we were in one of the most unique cities in the world. We did what most college boys did and will continue to do—we headed straight for the famous Lido Beach where we had a swim and planned a ride in a gondola in the evening.

My friend, John H. Davis, has recently published a beautiful picture book about Venice, *Venice: Art and Life in the Lagoon City*. In it he quotes some of the literature about Venice, what people say on visiting it for the first time, and excerpts from various authors who have used Venice as the setting for their works. Many of the great poets have also been inspired by Venice, including Shelley.

Mark Twain, in *Innocents Abroad*, described it as I remember seeing it that first time: "What a funny old city, this Queen of the Adriatic is! Narrow streets, vast gloomy marble palaces, black with the corroding damps of centuries, and all partly submerged. No dry land visible anywhere, and no sidewalks worth mentioning. If you want to go to church, to the theatre or to a restaurant, you must call a gondola. It must be a paradise for cripples, for verily a man has no use for legs here." It is obviously a way of life to which one must become accustomed.

The next few days in Venice consisted in seeing the sights all tourists have visited—the Doge's palace, the Bridge of Sighs, St. Mark's. Like most young men, what interested us most was meeting girls we could invite on a gondola. We also managed to work in another trip to the Lido so we could swim in the Adriatic. The gondoliers have always fascinated people over the years, and lovers of Gilbert and Sullivan never get tired of their romantic tale, "The Gondoliers," which has some of the most beautiful music Sullivan ever composed.

MORE PARIS

Venice was the climax of my own tour. Again, I took one of Europe's famous trains, the Simplon-Orient express, which went from Venice to Paris, where one saw beautiful scenery and the famous lake country of Italy. I felt very lonely in Paris, but did see a movie of the Dempsey-Carpentier fight. Jack Dempsey knocked the Frenchman out in four rounds.

The rest of my day in Paris was to see another French musical in a theatre that I think still exists, Les Ambassadeurs.

MORE LONDON

I found it was possible to fly to London, something I had always wanted to do. The plane turned out to be an old Handly-Page, with an open cockpit. I was a little scared but, when I got used to it, I really enjoyed myself. And it was nice to get back to London.

The following day, I was told that I had overdrawn my letter of credit. My father didn't say much, but I could see that he was disappointed in me for being so careless. It turned out, though, that it was a mistake of the banks involved and was corrected when we got back to New York but, for some time, I was under a cloud.

The days in London that followed my return were filled with sightseeing during the day and theatre at night. I was introduced to one other side of English life and that is the English club. I was taken to lunch at the Constitutional Club. I think it is no longer in existence, as I could not find it listed in a recent book of London clubs. One story is told about it: The secretary wrote to his opposite number at the Madras Club as follows: "Dear Sir: We have thirty of our members visiting India and would appreciate it if you would show them every hospitality. We cannot, of course, reciprocate, as you will readily understand." Sir Robert Dennison, secretary of the Madras Club, replied: "Dear Sir: I don't know much about the Constitutional Club except that it is of course some decades younger than the Madras Club. I asked one of the senior members if he could provide any information about your club, but he knew nothing about the Constitutional, except that he used to find it a useful place to raise a leg on the way to his own club.' "

That first luncheon was my introduction to English clubs, which I enjoyed greatly on the visits to London later in life.

I was particularly anxious to see top cricket and we went to see one of the test matches, England *vs.* Australia. Cricket is, of course, the most English of all games. I understood little of the game and its scoring, but I did enjoy the tremendous crowd and the great interest when an international match was played.

My father was particularly interested in the universities of England, and we made an excursion to Oxford. I remember thinking what a peaceful place it was, compared to the activity at Yale.

EDINBURGH AND MORE OF SCOTLAND AND ENGLAND

Our next excursion was to take the train to Edinburgh, which in those days took about nine hours. We arrived to find all the hotels filled so we stayed at a boarding house. The next day, I was again given the sightseeing treatment. Later in life, I have often repeated it whenever I went to a new city. I think taking the sightseeing bus is the best way to become familiar with a new city. I might say that I have never done this in my native New York City, but I should.

Edinburgh had two special places, as far as we were concerned, the University and the Castle up on the hill. The city did not impress me at the time. The highlight of the visit was to hear Harry Lauder, perhaps the greatest popular singer of his time. He was known all over the world and had a repertoire of songs that have become immortal, the most famous being "I Love a Lassie." Lauder was a music hall favorite in London, appearing there first in 1900. I had heard him before on one of his American tours, which were frequent. Bing Crosby and Frank Sinatra might be compared to Lauder as interpreters of the popular music of their time in our country.

On a very wet and cold day, we took a tour through the Scotch countryside and stopped at strange (for us) little inns for scotch whiskey. Our means of transportation was called a "charabanc," which is defined as "a long opened vehicle, typically an open motor coach, having several rows of seats extending across its width and facing forward."

We also made a trip to St. Andrews, the birthplace of golf. When I see it on television, when the British Open is played, it all comes back to me, the wonderful old clubhouse in a beautiful setting. I played the old course with one of the local pros. Comparing St. Andrews with other courses in the world, one would not find it very high up on the list, but none have the same aura about the game that exists here where the game began. I agree with what our great golf architect, Robert Trent Jones, said about St. Andrews: "The aspect from its first tee is not impressive nor is there any visible hint of its right to its honored position. Perhaps, one should never play the Old Course at St.

Andrews without first getting the spirit of the town. It is like no other town in the world. The very backbone of the town is golf, the spirit of the town is golf, and it is supported by its four golf courses, its beach and its University. The Royal and Ancient clubhouse lies but a block from the main street. Bordered by the sea, it sits there monumentally, a thing apart as it should be for the Royal and Ancient is the oldest and most respected Club in the world, celebrating its 200th season in 1954.''

In Edinburgh and wherever it was possible, we went to the theatre at night or to a music hall. The acting on stage in Britain has always been great. We saw a revival of William Gillette's old play, ''The Private Secretary.''

From Edinburgh, we went through the Trossachs, which is a valley in Central Scotland, on to Glasgow. There didn't seem to be much here for the tourist but my father wanted me to see the University.

We then started back toward London, our first stop being the old town of York, with its famous cathedral. In his magnificent book, *In Search of England*, published in 1927, long after our trip, H. V. Morton states: ''If you are interested in old things, in beautiful things and in the history of this country, there is one city, which will exceed your expectation—York.'' I spent the morning exploring the old town of York with its famous cathedral, just as Morton did. He wrote further, ''I walked round the Wall of York, which really looks like a town wall rejoicing in this peerless city.'' The big attraction is the cathedral or York Minster, as it is called. It is the only thing I remember and, as it has been said: ''From a distance York Minster dominates the city. It prints its magnificence on the eye and on the memory.''

I was told later that the cathedral contains two-thirds of the 14th Century glass in England. Later, in World War II in San Antonio, I had a friend in the Air Force whose hobby was stained glass windows in cathedrals, and he made me appreciate this art.

From York we went to Cambridge by train, which takes all day. This gave me the opportunity of seeing England's other great university town. Oxford and Cambridge have always been compared to Yale and Harvard in our own country. What impressed me about Cambridge most, I think, was its great beauty and atmosphere, unlike New Haven.

The best way to see anything is to take a guide, which we did. As was our habit, we went to the theatre in the evening, seeing a stock company performance of ''The Gypsy Princess.''

LONDON AGAIN

When we got back to London for my last week abroad, there was lots to do. My father wanted to see the famous cardiologist, Sir Thomas Lewis. Sir Thomas was one of the pioneers in electrocardiography. He was known all over the world for his basic research in this subject. My father took me with him, explaining that I would be a medical student at Columbia in the fall. Lewis' research laboratory was at the University College Hospital Medical School. We were cordially received, but found Sir Thomas a rather non-communicative man.

My last week in London was an eventful one from the standpoint of furthering my education. Theatre-going continued and I saw for the first time "The Grand Guignol." This consisted of several shocking short plays and ended with a farce, for comic relief. This type of production was well-known in Paris. We also saw "Bulldog Drummond," one of the most famous melodramas, which was later brought over to the U.S.A.

I heard that the great American court tennis player, Jay Gould, was to play against the English professional, Peter Latham. I had always had a great interest in court games, but I never thought at that time that I would later become a player myself. I went out to Queens Club, which is on the outskirts of London, to see the match. Gould beat Latham badly and my recollection is that, even though I didn't understand the game at all, certain things were of interest. First, the American player was very unpopular. When they would change sides, he would take a shot of whiskey. There also seemed to be a lack of sportsmanship in the match. The English gallery didn't seem to mind this, but were more fascinated by watching this amateur beat their great professional. It would be correct to say that, at the time, Gould was the greatest player in the world.

My last evening in London, I had dinner with my old schoolmaster, Francis Tabor, who had played such a significant role in my education at St. Bernard's School. This was the last time I would see him, as he died suddenly some years later.

On September 10, 1921, we took what was called the boat train to Liverpool, and sailed home on the S.S. Baltic. It turned out to be a very rough trip. Everyone seemed to be sick. Dramamine was not yet in use. It was a great thrill, after crossing the ocean, to see the lights of Coney Island. We were back in the U.S.A.

Chapter IX

Medical School

THE FAVORITE CAREER OF MANY OF MY FRIENDS at that time, where the most money and glamor existed, was in "The Street," where you began usually as a "runner." This is not "running" as we know it today. In those days, it meant delivering securities from one place to another. A second occupation there was to become a bond salesman for one of the brokerage houses. A few of the very affluent bought a seat on the stock exchange, which insured a good income. In a sense, this was like being elected to a good club and all that goes with it.

Wall Street was a pretty closed corporation when I was growing up. The Stock Exchange stopped trading at 3:00 p.m. Those brokers who were members of the Racquet Club would come up to the club after the exchange closed. It was actually a 10:00 a.m. to 3:00 p.m. job. The broker had a seat and an assured income—and that was that.

In my case, I went to medical school. September 28, 1921 was my first day in medical school. A recent graduate of medical school wrote a book about his experiences and, after reading it, I think the problems of medical students are the same in many aspects today as they were when I was a student sixty years ago.

My father had graduated from the same school I went to, the Columbia College of Physicians and Surgeons in New York. He had been a member of the second class to graduate, in 1889. The original school had been chartered in 1807 and was on 23rd Street and Fourth Avenue until it moved in 1887 to West 59th Street, just opposite Roosevelt Hospital. I also had heard that one of my ancestors, Dr. Louis Faugères, had been one of the founding fathers of what was the oldest medical school in new York.

With all this background, I was aware that I was expected to do well. It became apparent to me very quickly that graduate school is not college. There are a few similarities, such as the fraternities, and the small groups that band together to study, but the general atmosphere is entirely different.

Everyone is there for one purpose and one purpose only, and

that is to study medicine, get their M.D. after four years of study, to be followed by what was then called an "internship" in a hospital. Competition for the good hospitals was fierce and the better your marks at P&S, the better your chances for a good spot after graduation.

Great emphasis was put on scholarship and, if you didn't do well scholastically, you stood a good chance of being thrown out. In our class, which numbered a little over one hundred, this did actually occur to about ten percent.

Whereas there was a small group of privileged students, ranging from moderate circumstances to rich, of which I was one, the majority had come to P&S at great sacrifice from their families. With the large Jewish population in New York, I think about seventy percent of the class were Jewish. Women were not admitted to P&S until 1917, but we did have a small number of women students. This was my first encounter with female fellow students since kindergarten. At the present time, practically all schools are coeducational, even Yale.

P&S was housed in an old barn-like building. It consisted of classrooms, laboratories of various kinds and, on the top floor, was the dissecting room where we were taught anatomy. On the ground floor was a coatroom which was run by a pair of characters who knew every student and knew all the inside gossip about the school.

Results of examinations were posted in the front hall from time to time. We came there trembling and full of fear to see our marks as it was a very serious matter to flunk a course.

Classes and laboratory work in the preclinical years ran from nine to five, except that Saturday and Sunday were free. I also remember there was a small library where it was possible to study if you had any free time. This rarely occurred, as the day was completely filled with lectures and laboratory work.

As far as lunch was concerned, there were a number of places to go around Columbus Circle, which was close by. Many students brought their lunch with them, but I was not one of these. The famous Child's Restaurant, which at that time played a big part in the night life of New York, was one of the favorite spots. There was no inflation at the time and a cup of coffee was five cents. Columbus Circle also was the site of the famous Reisenwebber's, where I went during my college days. Along with other cabarets of the time, it has disappeared from the area.

It is a custom in most medical schools to have various types of indoctrination where you meet the faculty. The first one of these took place at the P&S Club. Here, members of the faculty gave us some advice on how to be a medical student. They were all distinguished members of the faculty and well known names in medicine at the time, such as Wilcox, Van Buren and St. John.

We were told that our first two years at P&S were to be essentially in the preclinical sciences, which included anatomy, physiology, chemistry, and bacteriology. We would not have contact with patients. At the present time, I believe that this has changed and the student gets into practical medicine much earlier.

The dean of the school at this time was Dr. William Darrach. He was a surgeon and had had a distinguished military career in World War I. He had taken this position in 1919 and had a lot to do with the new medical center when P&S moved to its new location at 168th Street. As a student, I saw very little of the dean, but remember him as a kindly gentleman.

In *A Biographical History of the College of Physicians and Surgeons*, published by the Alumni Association of the College of Physicians and Surgeons, it was said of Dr. Darrach that, "He accomplished much to smooth the passage for P&S from a self-contained academic institution to a partner in an administrative complex venture with far-reaching clinical and scholarly implications." All of this had begun when I started at P&S, but it didn't mean much to us at the time. Our world was 59th Street, and most of us would never see the new medical center that did not open officially until 1928. Dr. Darrach resigned as dean in 1930.

In the first month, we were invited to the two medical fraternities that existed at the time, one of which was Chi Phi and the other Nu Sigma Nu. Should I be asked, the best one for me was Nu Sig, as it was called. I still remembered the Yale experience, although it didn't seem to me that a medical school fraternity was of any great importance. It turned out to be of more importance than I thought. The fraternities gave me closer contact with other students than I might have had otherwise.

I have a picture, dated January 26, 1922, of our chapter of Nu Sigma Nu. We used to meet at Keen's Chophouse, which has recently been renovated. It is a wonderful picture of the interior of the chandeliered and pillared chophouse and the banquet that we had there. Seated around the table are a number of my close friends of that era. One was Andy Hoyt, whom I used to walk to school with, and alongside of me, Bob Wise, who later became a famous surgeon. All of my close friends in my class

Dr. William Darrach, Dean, Columbia University, Physician and Surgeons Medical School.

Iota Chapter, Nu Sigma Nu. Keens, January 26, 1922.

are in this picture: Dave Moore, Len Moore, as well as Dr. Don Carson. In the background is Dr. Burton Opitz, the famous professor, who became active later in the New York Cardiological Society.

The first term at P&S included studies in anatomy, where we had to memorize the various details of the bones of the body with the aid of what I suppose is the most famous of all medical school text books, *Gray's Anatomy.* I do not know if it is used any more, but in those days, it was like a Bible. The first bone given to me for some reason or other was the scapula. The scapula is described as the shoulder blade, "a large triangular flattened bone lying over the ribs posteriorly on either side, articulating by its outer angle with the clavicle and the humerus." This all had to memorized.

It could take a whole evening to learn about one bone. It is no easy matter to note down and memorize the details of the bones of the body and then give it back in a classroom, particularly as we were not, and even more particularly I was not, used to studying this hard.

I did not consider that I was very adept, but we had teachers, called prosectors, who helped us, so we could learn anatomy.

A second course in the first months was in physiology. Physiology is defined as a science which deals with "living things, with the normal vital processes of animal and vegetable organisms." It was taught by a friend of my father's, Dr. Burton

Opitz. Although I didn't know it at the time, he was to become a friend of mine long after I graduated.

I realized that, up until medical school, I had really not known how to study. Each night there were three or four hours hard studying. You might have an occasional evening off or a weekend off but, for the most part, the amount of study that had to be carried out was tremendous. I was about in the middle of the class as far as grades were concerned.

It has been said, and I think it is as true today as it was in 1921, that students experience intense loneliness when they try to master mountains of material. They feel inadequate and useless. Many times, we questioned our decision to become physicians. Today, medical students are better prepared on the undergraduate level than we were then. I also felt that I had not mastered the art of studying and that I did not always pay attention to what was going on, but would let my mind wander. In my diary, I wrote: "Concentrate and develop this power as it is a big aid to success."

We students began to study together, which we had never done in college. I found out that it is not only an advantage but

Columbia, P&S Medical School. Anatomy Class.

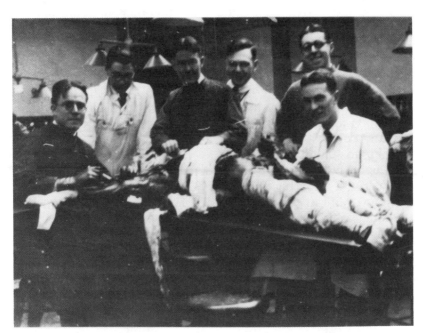

a necessity to study with someone to prepare for tests, which were frequent. I and one of my friends, Simon Beisler, who had been at Yale, frequently did this during the first year. I also found out that many of the students had been given copies of various future tests by upper class students. Fortunately or unfortunately, I did not know any upperclassmen.

One thing was certain. I needed some good friends to survive these first two years, because of the very competitive atmosphere that existed at P&S and that exists in all professional schools. However, good friends are hard to come by. One or two had come to P&S from Yale, but no more.

At this point, I was lucky to meet Andy Hoyt, whom I had known slightly at Yale, and who would become my close friend at P&S over the next four years. We helped each other and I have often wondered if I would have gotten through without him.

Andy was a most charming fellow of good intellect. He was older than I, and came from a very rich family, who lived in what seemed to be a castle on Park Avenue. It contained a squash court, which greatly impressed me. It was the antithesis of where one would expect the average medical student to make his home. At that time, my family lived on 72nd Street, between Park and Lexington, and Andy would stop for me every morning, and we would walk to school across the park, talking as we walked. We spent much time together and, the more I knew him, the more I admired him and was inspired by him.

The first few months were very difficult for me. I was no different from many others, but I think I had more outside attractions. I gradually realized that there would be little time for them. I continued to frequent the theatre, I kept up a program of exercise and kept in touch with my old friends. Being at an age which my mother called "the mating season," I was asked to many debutante parties.

Going to school in New York, where I had some good friends from college, and where I was also now established in the social world, I quickly learned that I would have to lead a very disciplined life to survive. I lived at home, which had some disadvantages but a great deal of comfort.

It was evident that I was not spending enough time on my studies. I had already heard from my preceptor that, in general, my marks were not satisfactory. I wrote in my diary at that time the following platitude: "Time is a queer and important element in one's life. Don't waste it, whatever you do or if it goes, you can't get it back again. Use your head. Think. Keep your eyes open and work. The motto of a successful life."

It has been said that the four-year education that turns a layman into a physician is dotted with symbolic milestones. After our study of the dry bones, which had involved long periods of discipline and, in particular, a good memory, sometime in November we eventually started dissection. I believe there was some arrangement with the city whereby the school obtained human bodies from the city morgue. The dissection of a cadaver made me realize that the study of anatomy would take on a new dimension. In a sense, this could be considered a milestone.

The first day in the dissection room, where you encountered, on stone-covered dissecting tables, the heavily embalmed cadavers, is an experience a medical student does not forget.

There was a then well-known surgeon named Erdman, who had a son at school; the son was going to succeed his father in the surgical practice. The first day that we had a dissection class and all these bodies laid out before us, young Erdman took one look, turned around, left the building and, as far as I know, never returned.

As a matter of fact, it was hard on many of us. But in time, it became just a part of our studies.

In our school, one body was assigned to two students and I found myself working with Simon Beisler. We would have the same body for dissection for the next few months.

The idea of this course in dissection is to lay bare the human body, painstakingly exploring and recognizing every minute nerve, organ, and bone. It is a time-consuming and tedious process, and also involves patience and a prodigious memory. Of course, we followed the textbook, *Gray's Anatomy*, and we were helped by the young instructors in the anatomy department. Although I was not and never have been good at the mechanical end, which, in a sense, involved some of the techniques used by surgeons, I found it interesting. And it seemed to me, and I think also to my fellow students, we were on our way to becoming doctors of medicine. I think the dissecting room, in a sense, gave us a feeling of superiority, that we had the privilege of learning about the human body.

These early days in the dissecting room were long and hard. A typical day for me would be 7:30 to 10:00, dissection; 10:00 to 1:00, chemistry; 2:00 to 5:00, physiology; lecture 5:00 to 6:00. I would exercise by fencing until 7:15, then have dinner and then study from 9:00 to 2:00. I am sure medical school for all students in the first year is something like this.

I did not do as well that first year as I had hoped and this made it necessary for me to work very hard. It made me realize that my education would never stop and, no matter what field of medicine I would finally be a part of, I would continue always to be a student. If I had had an easy time of it, this lesson would not have been impressed on me. There is no doubt that every doctor, throughout his medical life, is aware of the challenge of keeping up and, today, postgraduate courses and symposiums are a part of all medical associations and institutions.

At summer holiday that first year, many of my fellow students had to work through the summer. I realized that I was privileged to have nothing to do but enjoy the social life at the seashore.

The second year at P&S was much like the first with the exception that I had learned how to study and I now had a number of good friends, many of whom I would continue to know throughout my medical life. That second year we were introduced to some new subjects and also new professors. P&S had a very eminent faculty. Our study of anatomy continued. It seemed to us that we would never finish with this and, as a matter of fact, I don't think we ever did.

Anatomy is one of the most difficult of the medical courses, but eventually I did pass. Again, so much had to be memorized. The professor of anatomy had the distinguished name of Huntington. My only recollection of him was that he looked like a professor. His lectures were on comparative anatomy and embryology, involving the heart. For the most part, it was completely over our heads, but we listened, realizing the importance of the man.

On a more practical level was the subject of bacteriology, to which we were introduced. The definition of bacteriology is "the branch of science which has to do with the study of unicellular vegetable organisms and with their relation to medicine, agriculture, and the arts." Obviously, we were interested in the medical aspects of the subject. Dr. Hans Zinsser not only was a famous scientist, but later was to write a classic book. We all respected him as a teacher. I had a particular interest in him as he was one of a family that were great friends of my mother but, as a teacher, he gave me no special consideration. He was such a fine teacher and presented his course so well, that no one had much difficulty with it. In addition to bacteriology, we were introduced to the broad subject of public health.

Neurology was another subject that was brought to our attention. Neurology is the branch of medical science which has to do with the nervous system and its disorders. It was taught to us by a brilliant younger man, Dr. Byron Stookey, and an exciting thing happened. For the first time, we were presented with

Six Department Heads appointed during Dean Lambert's Tenure. (**Top row, left to right**) *Warfield T. Longcope, Medicine; Adrian V. S. Lambert, Surgery; Hans Zinsser, Bacteriology.* (**Bottom**) *Frederick Tilney, Neurology; James W. Jobling, Pathology; J. Bentley Squier, Urology.*

a real live patient, our first case. It is hard to believe the good effect this had on our class. This was the first of many neurological problems we would see. And we were very grateful, after our long period with nothing but basic science.

We were introduced at this point to pathology. Perhaps the broadest of all medical subjects, it is defined as "the branch of medical science which deals with disease in all its relations, especially with its nature and the functional and material changes caused by it.'' Besides this major course, we were gradually introduced to other subjects, and for the first time I heard a lecture in psychiatry, by Professor Salmon, who was at the time one of the well-known men in this field.

Pharmacology was another new subject which required a lot of memory. Pharmacology is a branch of science which has to do with drugs and all their relations. Some of our class had worked in pharmacies, or drugstores, as they were called, and had some advantages from the practical side of this difficult subject.

About this time, the subject of physical diagnosis entered our lives, something we would be doing, if we were to enter the practice of medicine, the rest of our lives. With the aid of an instructor, we practiced on our fellow students.

Besides our regular routine work, many of us would go over across the street and watch from a gallery some of the operations that were being done at Roosevelt Hospital. As a matter of fact, we got very little education from this, but we felt that we were now qualified to be a close part of the medical profession. We also continued to attend all the autopsies we could and we were notified when and where they would be taking place.

About this time a strange fellow, or so we thought him at the time, gave a course in some of the basic principles of surgery. His name was Dr. W. C. Clark and he was sort of a philosopher. For some reason or other, he would decide whether one had good reasoning power. He decided I had not and, as a result, at the end of the year, I was flunked and had to take another exam in the fall. My recollection of the course was that it was not a very definite subject, but an abstract approach to surgery.

Bill Clark, as I believe he was called, flunked me in his surgical course and said I had to take a make-up exam in the fall if I were to continue in medical school. In his opinion—and he may have been right—I needed more discipline and, as I realize now, I was young, even for a medical student in his second year.

What he suggested was that I work in the Presbyterian Hospital surgical clinic for the summer. This consisted in helping out in the clinic and doing, as I was allowed, a little minor surgery. Clark also gave me several books on surgery, of a somewhat philosophical nature. I had no feeling that I would fail in the fall, but it had the effect of keeping me worried, which is not so good for a summer vacation following the gruelling second term in medical school.

At the time, I felt I had been done wrong by Clark. But, in

retrospect, I think he did the right thing. My life at this time was fun and games and I needed this extra work if I were going to succeed.

Thus, the first part of our second year ended with exams, which never gave any of us a chance to ease up from long hours of study. The climax was the final exam in gross anatomy, which we had a terrible fear we could never pass. As a matter of fact, we all did. But there is nothing worse than the worry a young medical student goes through over examinations.

Presbyterian Hospital was at that time near where we lived on upper Park Avenue and convenient to me. At Presbyterian, where I worked in the mornings, was a surgeon named Carp, who was very nice to me. I think his name was Louis Carp, and I found out later that he was one of the best in New York. I tried, during the summer of 1923, besides working at the clinic, to study what Clark had suggested, but it was difficult. At all events, the exam finally came toward the end of September. I passed. This made it certain in my mind that I would graduate.

What does a medical student do when he is not in school, particularly in the summer? There is no doubt that during the school year, any social activity is bought at a great sacrifice. But the summer is a different matter, even if you have some sort of job.

The summer of '23, except for working in the clinic at Presbyterian, I was on my own and life was one continuous pleasure-seeking adventure.

Although I didn't think much about it at the time, my life was far easier than many of my fellow students, because of family support. I lived at home and the word "rent" was not one I was familiar with. My mother furnished clothes when I needed them, and saw that I had sufficient spending money to be "on the town." There was always dinner at home, if I chose.

Many of my college friends were in New York and available to have fun with. There was an expression then, which is still used, and that is "to sow your wild oats." This was certainly part of our life the summer of '23. We seemed always to have an automobile available, usually borrowed from one of our families, which enabled us to get around, wherever we wanted to go. Unlike today, the cost of living was low and, if you had any money, it went very far.

The "in" night club was the Montmartre. It was on Broadway and that was where we took girls in the evening to dance. This was usually followed by supper at Reuben's, which was famous for its sandwiches. This type of evening, with the so-called upper class girls we knew, consisted of dancing, talk and very limited sex, if at all. This was how we "dated" at the time.

During that summer, Christy Emmet and I drove out to the North Shore to play golf and to spend the night with his family. This was my first introduction to Piping Rock Club, which still exists as one of America's great country clubs. In the twenties, it was synonymous with the richest and highest social status in the world. The Emmet family were members and Christy and I were allowed to use it.

Many years later, I became a member and, although there are many changes in the social structure, the club is still famous, as it was then, for its sporting activity, particularly golf and tennis. Polo, which was a part of life in the twenties, is no more, although there seems to be renewed interest at this time in some parts of the country. Then, polo was played on a field right in front of the main clubhouse, which is now used as a practice range for golf.

The theatre continued to be one of my loves, and that summer there were many big musicals on Broadway. We saw them all, including the Follies, The Music Box Revue and the Vanities. One of the producers of the Vanities was a friend of mine and allowed us to see rehearsals of the shows before they opened. The stars were Joe Cook, the comedian, and the famous Peggy Hopkins Joyce. I vaguely remember a song in the show called "Pretty Peggy."

Broadway is still thriving, but the great era of musical comedies and revues is no more. There were also great dramatic plays then and I recall an impressive production of the Theatre Guild called "Devil's Disciple," starring Basil Sydney and Roland Young.

Games were an important part of my life and I had been elected a member of the Racquet & Tennis Club, where I could play squash, which I loved. In addition, I was able to get away weekends to play golf, either at Easthampton or in Connecticut, where my friend Ingersoll lived. The Racquet membership at that time consisted mostly of brokers and various types who worked on Wall Street. As a medical student, I was sort of a unique specimen. Nevertheless, because I loved to play, it was easy to get a game or play with one of the professionals whenever I went there.

Probably the most luxurious club for games in the world, it has changed very little since the summer of 1923. I was interested to compare the cost of food at the club in 1923 to today. A small steak, which was my favorite dish then as it is now, cost $1.75, as compared with $13.50 today. That is quite a difference, even allowing that money was worth more then.

Another activity I enjoyed that summer was that of sports spectator. At that time, boxing was big in New York and it was possible to see many fights, not only in the heavyweight division, where Dempsey was the best in the world, but the light-weights, who included some of the all-time greats, such as Benny Leonard and Lou Tendler. I rarely missed a fight.

It was also the summer when the greatest heavyweight bout in boxing history took place and there has never been anything like it since. I was a long way from ringside, but it will never be forgotten by anyone who was there. Dempsey KO'd Luis Firpo, but not before he had been knocked out of the ring himself. No one who saw the fight remembers how many rounds, how many knockdowns or anything else. It has been fun in later life to say that I was there. I remember it took place at the Polo Grounds and it was a very cold night in the fall.

Another interest that summer was music and it was possible to hear the Philharmonic, which played at Lewisohn Stadium. One of my friends was a music lover and we went up often. At the time, I did not realize it, but it is important to expose your-self to classical music at an early age, because you can continue to enjoy it the rest of your life, which has been true in my case.

The summer also included a trip to Newport. Newport was then the richest and most social summer resort in America and so-called eligible young men were sought after. My friend and I were invited. We went up by boat, which was one of the ways of getting there at that time. We usually travelled around in pairs, probably as a form of self-preservation.

Amateur tennis was the big social game, and one of the major tournaments was held at the Newport Casino. We arrived in time to see some of it. Although I never played lawn tennis, it was a spectator sport that I loved to watch, even more than I do professional tennis, as it is played today.

Of course, we had to attend one of Newport's balls, which was one of the reasons we had been asked. This was an era of lavish entertainment, the like of which has not been seen since.

We paid a visit to Bailey's Beach, a name known throughout the world as the most exclusive beach. At the time I remember it looked rather "crummy" to me compared to the beaches on Long Island, where I had spent summers when I was growing up.

There was also an opportunity to play golf at the Newport Country Club, where an unfortunate accident occurred. I failed to call "fore" and I hit one of the members in the back, for which he reported me although he was not hurt. It was unpleasant for our hostess, but it didn't spoil our trip. I was requested not to play again, but it was unlikely, as we left for New York that night.

I don't think the sex life of a medical student was any different from what it was for any other 22-year-old man. During the school year, we were limited as far as devoting time to its pursuit was concerned, and we were fearful of emotional involvements, as our careers might be jeopardized. The summer was different. Commercial sex was always around but did not interest me or my friends. In the twenties, there was not the permissive society that exists today, but there were girls who would let you sleep with them, particularly those who worked and had their own apartments. Unfortunately, in my case, I became very attached to one and, when our romance ended after the summer, it was hard on both of us.

I returned to medical school for my third year. The second two years, called the "clinical years," were when we were taught about disease. The atmosphere and pressure at P&S was very different. We had finished the preclinical or basic science and we were more certain now of graduating. We were given courses taught by practicing specialists with real patients. Even at this early stage, we could see which aspects of medicine particularly interested us and in which we thought we might specialize in the distant future.

It was obvious we would be influenced by the professor who taught us. What was different from the present time was that those who taught us, beside teaching, were in private practice, so we were able to learn more about this than the student of today, who rarely encounters the private practitioner.

The subjects, in addition to medicine and surgery, which included formal lectures as well as case presentations, included pediatrics, dermatology, ophthalmology, psychiatry, urology and syphilology, clinical pathology and obstetrics. We were given textbooks in these subjects, often written by our own professors. Although I studied hard, it was interesting and the pressure was off. It seemed as if every day of this third year was exciting.

Sometime in this year I was elected to the "Omega Club." I was never quite sure what this organization, which had existed for some time, meant. I am not sure whether it still exists. I was first told that the Omega Club elected only superior students but this certainly did not seem to apply to me. It apparently was there when Omega was considered a sort of elite group that might go somewhere in the future. At this late date, I am not sure just what it was, but the Omega Club meant a great deal to the students at P&S.

I have thought a lot lately about the clinical years, or the third and fourth years at P&S, where we were exposed to the clinical teaching of the specialties. I realize now that we could only get a glimpse of what a "specialist" was and those who taught could only tell us a little in the short course given. Yet, the stature of the men who taught was so great, that many of us who were to be influenced would try to follow in their footsteps.

Who were the men that I remember? First, there was a psychiatrist, with the peculiar name of Cassamajor. I believe he was called Cassy. He gave us a series of lectures in psychiatry, which at that time was not a popular subject, and yet he was so good a teacher that our class hung on every word he said. These were formal lectures and were not accompanied by live patients.

Neurology was another subject that we had a taste of. Dr. E. Livingston Hunt was the professor. For this course, we had to travel to one of the city hospitals, I think it was Metropolitan. At one of his clinics, I remember that he showed a number of his patients who had different gaits. By watching them walk, he demonstrated how it was possible to make a clinical diagnosis. For example, a patient with *paralysis agitans* or syphilitic disease or *tabes dorsalis* has a gait which is classical of the disease. Even today, when I see someone on the street with a peculiar gait, I remember this clinical lesson that I had as a student.

Then, there was the rather affluent specialist who taught urology. We admired the way he dressed and that he had a car and chauffeur. He was a giant in his field and his name was J. Bentley Squier. He eventually had a building named after him at P&S. The amount of urology we absorbed, I think, was very little, but we were impressed with the importance of prostatic surgery which, in those days, carried extreme risk, even the hands of very competent surgeons. It is different today and, although prostate surgery is still not without danger, as is any surgery, it is far safer than it was then.

Dermatology lent itself well to this type of teaching. We could see a large number of patients with various skin diseases in the clinic and have their characteristics pointed out to us by the professors. One was Fordyce and another, named Rosen, were so good and made it so interesting that many of us thought this specialty was for us. It seemed one saw a lot of patients, treatment was not too difficult and one could expect a good income. At the time, I was not thinking that often there would be little that could be done to cure these diseases. Syphilis was a common problem and we saw many cases of syphilitic rash.

Of course, after each new course, we would decide that that was the specialty to be pursued.

Some of the other sub-specialties were, perhaps, not as dramatic. One was ENT, ear, nose and throat. At that time, before the advent of ear surgery, there were no ear specialists. Our textbook was written by Copley, who had a big ENT practice. We were taught how to examine the nose and throat, how to treat the problems. One of the common operations was tonsillectomy, which is not done routinely today. We learned how to perform it and that was good practice for those who intended to go into surgery. We learned how to examine the ear. Mastoiditis was quite common. Not so today, with the introduction of antibiotics, which were unheard of, unthought of, in 1925. Infections were far more serious than at the present time. One of the great changes brought out by the historians of medicine is that now the infections can be controlled.

The last year at medical school was spent in as much contact with patients interspersed with lectures as it was possible to give us in the hospitals with which P&S was associated. We worked as clinical clerks at Bellevue and Presbyterian, where we were assigned to wards, where we were allowed to examine the patients and do histories and physicals, which were later checked by the interns and attending physicians.

For the first time, you began to feel that you were really into medicine: seeing, examining, taking care of patients, discussing your diagnosis and treatment of the particular problem. Bellevue Hospital was unique because every type of disease was present. It was possible that there, as a fourth year medical student, you would see problems that you would probably never see again in your lifetime.

The professor of obstetrics was Dr. Howard Taylor. I remember him as an impressive, well-dressed man, who seemed always to have just delivered a Vanderbilt or an Astor and never failed to mention it. Today, mentioning patients by name would not be very ethical. After one of his lectures where he described the course of a delivery, he asked for questions. One of our class ventured to ask, "Is it painful to have a baby?" He had apparently been asleep and wanted to say something. The professor never batted an eye but, after a studied pause, replied, "Did you ever pass a watermelon?" which, as they say in show biz, brought down the house.

We were all expected to deliver a certain number of babies to fulfill the requirements of graduation and, I believe, a state law. We were, therefore, sent to a poor Italian or Jewish home on the Lower East Side where usually the mother had had a number of babies before the one we were supposed to deliver. A visiting nurse or midwife took charge. We were told what to do and it usually was a pleasant experience. Babies are usually slippery when they are born and I was always afraid of dropping them, as I was never too good at holding on to things. If any trouble arose, we had to get an obstetrician on the scene as soon as possible, but this was very rare. The help that we gave was appreciated by these poor families and we were often given wine or a little something to eat after the birth. When we consider milestones of our medical education, none is more exciting than the experience of delivering a baby for the first time. There is an emotional impact in watching a new life begin.

I think we, as medical students, were beginning to realize that we were no longer free, having chosen medicine as a profession. We were formed by the rules of our profession and a standard of conduct that had been impressed upon us. The pattern had been predetermined.

I remember that when we got close to graduation, you began to take pains to look like a doctor. You did this by wearing the white coats worn by the doctors in the hospitals and you also carried conspicuously your stethoscope around your neck and in your pocket to tell the world that you were a doctor. We all did this.

In those days, it seems to me, you were closer to the patient than you are today. One reason perhaps is that there was much less technology and fewer laboratory tests available. A good deal depended on your ability to get a good history, examining and talking to the patient. We also did many of the procedures ourselves, such as examining the urine or doing a blood count. Today, tests are done in the laboratory with very sophisticated equipment. Even the electrocardiogram was new at that time. So much has taken place in the past fifty years from the technological standpoint and this has, I think, taken away from so-called bedside medicine. As I think back to my days at medical school, we were taught over and over again, the importance of the physical examination.

At that time, we became aware for the first time of the terrible toll of drug addiction. Drug addiction is not a new phenomenon. We saw many heroin users, often infected with malaria as well from "mainlining." As I have said before, no one was turned away from Bellevue.

In writing about my teachers at P&S I can only quote what Oliver Wendell Holmes wrote in *Our Hundred Days in Europe* about that time. Toward the end of his life, when he returned to Paris, where he had been a student, he says, "How strange it is to look down on one's venerated teachers after climbing with world's progress half a century above the level where we left them. This is the feeling I had in writing about the medical school days. 'Nous avons changé tout cela' is true of every generation in medicine—changed often times by improvement, sometimes by fashion, or the pendulum swing from one extreme to the other."

We were all thinking about where we would like to intern. The usual thing at the time was to serve a two-year internship before starting to practice, which was considered more than sufficient for the average man going into the practice of medicine. An internship in New York in 1925, the year we would graduate, was highly competitive, and was obtained in practically every instance by examination, usually both written and oral. This was very different from the present day, where internships are determined by the schools by a somewhat complicated matching system. I am not quite sure how it works.

I first took the Roosevelt Hospital exams, where I thought I had a good chance, but, after it was all over, I found I did not make it. In this type of competition, you either win or lose and, because I had wanted this appointment very much, it was a big disappointment. St. Luke's Hospital, where I had a family connection, and one of the great hospitals for an intern, was not interested in my application for examination. They did not believe in married interns, something I expected to be after graduation. My next try was Bellevue Hospital, which did not have a medical school affiliation. It is now affiliated with N.Y.U. I was well aware that Bellevue was the most famous of all hospitals and a byword to millions who had never laid eyes on it.

The Bellevue examination for internship was presided over by Dr. Charles Nammack and Dr. Alexander Lambert. It was open to all comers who might want to work at Bellevue Hospital and consisted of a written examination which was followed by an oral. Following these, which occurred on two separate days, all the candidates were assembled in an auditorium where the results were announced for the various appointments.

The two-year jobs in medicine and surgery were considered the best, consisting of six months in pathology, six months in surgery and a year on the medical service if you accepted a medical appointment. If you wanted to be a surgeon, you took a year in surgery and six months in medicine. You could start in July or January, which meant there were four top places to be given to the contestants. There were also other types of internship, involving a lesser period of time, but everyone, it seemed to me, was only interested in the two-year jobs. The written examination didn't seem to be difficult to me at the time, but when it is competitive, there is plenty to worry about. The same with the oral exam—it matters a good deal how you impress the examiner and we were all well aware of this.

As far as I was concerned, the results were dramatic. I received the two-year appointment in medicine in January 1926, which was exactly what I wanted, as I would take the summer months off to get married before starting my internship.

There are days in your life that you can never forget and this was one for me. I can even remember the weather—it was a grey cold day, such as New York can have early in December. To hear my name called as winner of the competitive examination gave me a thrill such as I don't think I had ever had before. Actually, I think there was a tie for first and second place, which made little difference as I wanted the January appointment and not July. I did not know that a good part of my early medical life following my internship would be spent on the wards and clinics of Bellevue Hospital.

It is all different at the present time. The medical student is evaluated by the school and its dean's letter goes forward to the hospital. Nearly every medical student gets one of the preferred hospitals of his choice. It has been described as a seller's market for students seeking house staff positions. Hospitals now pay a salary, where, in my day, it was bed and board—and you were lucky to get that.

Following receiving my appointment to Bellevue Hospital, and the rest of my class also having received their hospital appointments, the pressure was off. Unless you did something terrible and started failing everything, nothing could happen between this point and graduation. Your M.D. was assured.

Graduation from medical school is somewhat of an anticlimax and really only of interest to the family. Yours was only one of many post-graduate schools. If you attended the ceremony, you were asked to stand and that was it. Your M.D. degree was mailed to you at home, eventually. I found out later I had won a prize in pediatrics, a subject in which I didn't have any particular interest.

Of course, we were all happy to be graduating and the diploma was the important thing, but it seemed strange that, after all the very hard work of four years, you sort of tiptoed out and there was very little ceremony.

Chapter X

Celebrities

AFTER COLLEGE, WHILE AT MEDICAL SCHOOL, my close friend, Ralph Ingersoll, continued to be my roommate. He had just begun to work for the *New Yorker*. No one at that time could foresee the future of this now world-famous magazine, nor that those associated with it would become celebrities. At the time, it was a question of whether I would get through medical school, and whether Ingersoll and the *New Yorker* would survive, but nevertheless, we did try to keep up with this extraordinary group of people by frequent theatre-going and we were invited to many parties, both organized and unorganized. A medical student was a bit of an oddity.

From time to time, Ralph and I were asked to join the now historic round table group at the Algonquin. We liked them, they liked us and we never thought about their future role in American literary life and the theatre. None of them had any money.

Alexander Woollcott was older than we and was fairly well-known as a critic. Critics wielded more power then than they do now, I think. When one asked someone between the acts how they liked the play, the joke answer was, "How do I know, I haven't read the critics."

Katie and Sig Spaeth frequently invited us to their apartment on the upper West Side. They often entertained. He later became known as the "Tune Detective" on radio, but at that time he worked for a piano company. He had tremendous knowledge of music and many musicians were attracted to their parties. I remember one party where George Gershwin was playing the piano and was asked to stop, because it was interfering with the conversation.

It was a great time to be young in New York, and we met many other young people who went on to play important roles and to be successful.

Another drama critic of the day was Heywood Broun, well-known to the round table. He later became important in other fields and covered both sports and political conventions. As a

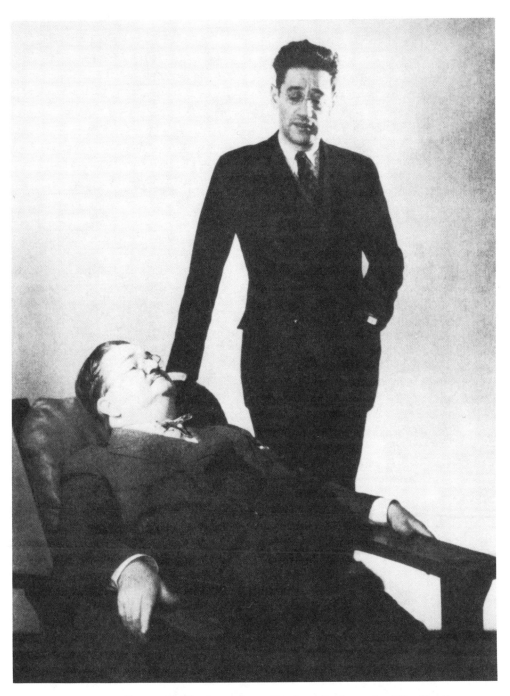

George S. Kaufman (standing) *and Alexander Woollcott.*

Lillian Hellman, the author of 'The Children's Hour, one of the most literate, sensitive, and human dramas in the contemporary theatre.

young squash player at the Racquet & Tennis Club, of which he was a member, I saw him frequently in the dressing room, usually when he was recovering from a late night. I remember him as a great big man who was usually described by his friends as looking as if he had just got out of bed. I never thought of him as a celebrity, which he was. It seemed strange to me that, although he was considered far to the left politically, he was a very popular member of a conservative bastion such as the Racquet.

We also saw Ruth Hale, Broun's wife, from time to time. She was one of the early women's libbers, the militant president of the Lucy Stone League. It was their policy not to use husband's names.

My connection with Harold Ross, the editor of the *New Yorker*, was very slight. Ingersoll told me he was a genius and I accepted his opinion. I was told that Ross was a hypochondriac but he had no interest in a medical student like me. I remember him as a young man whose hair stood almost straight up. He had almost everyone in the literary world of that time working for him, including me, when, for a time, I helped with a column on court games, which was a brain child of Geoffrey Hellman's.

Recently, one of the most brilliant of our American playwrights, Lillian Hellman, sat at a table near to my wife and me at Sardi's. We waved and I spoke to her, "Do you remember the early days when we saw a lot of each other?" She was a good friend of Ingersoll's and we went to many of the same parties. Seeing her brought back my first impressions of this remarkable woman. I remember, during the time when I first knew her, Ingersoll told me that of all the writers he knew, she was the most clear-headed and best organized. At that time, Lillian Hellman was a press agent, a play reader and a book reviewer. She had not yet written any plays. Her first, "The Children's Hour," appeared in 1934, long after the time we first knew her in New York.

When I would question Ingersoll about his great admiration for her during that time when she had not yet begun her work in the theatre, his answer was always the same: "Listen to her talk. She understands the use of words. When she talks to me, it is like listening to great music."

I had one professional contact with Lillian Hellman. When she was writing one of her greatest plays, "The Little Foxes" (which, incidentally, made a star of Tallulah Bankhead), Lillian Hellman wanted to kill off one of her characters with a heart attack and I told her how this might be dramatically presented (and be medically correct) provided the character was known to have heart disease. My advice was actually used in the play. I was flattered that she had asked me. The play appeared in 1939 and, like everything else she did, was a great success. Elizabeth Taylor made her Broadway debut in this play not long ago.

Across from where I live now on 63rd Street, is a house which was owned by Gypsy Rose Lee before she died. When Ingersoll and I knew her in the early thirties, no one could have predicted her rise to international fame in the theatre. We used to frequent the old Irving Place Theatre, which, at that time, was devoted to burlesque. Besides the star attraction and the other girls, there were standup comics, and many of our well-known comedians got their training in burlesque. Because it was close to Bellevue Hospital, the Irving was a popular spot with the interns who worked there.

The strip tease has probably existed in one form or another for centuries, but Gypsy presented a technique entirely her own. She would appear fully dressed, including long gloves and, then, to accompanying music, she would proceed to remove everything in a ladylike, dignified way. She was a tall, dark, beautiful girl and her act would pack this downtown theatre whenever she played there.

My friend Ingersoll, who used to go with me, decided that he wanted to write a piece on burlesque and so, because of this, we got to know the management and the performers. This involved inviting Gypsy to a night club for further consultation. There we learned that she was the girl friend of Dutch Schultz, the gangster. From that evening on, we never saw her again, except on stage.

Lunching recently with an old friend, I asked him if he remembered Gypsy Rose Lee. Like all of us, he remembered the way she always began, by removing those long gloves. Gypsy was unique. She had class!

One other interesting thing happened during our burlesque days. One of the girls in the show was pregnant. The rumor was that the father was a member of Congress and the romance had blossomed when the troupe had appeared in Washington some months before.

A friend of mine wanted to adopt the baby of this union, particularly as the mother was a beautiful, as well as intelligent, Polish girl. I, in my medical capacity, was to arrange it. The baby was to be born at Bellevue, where I worked; the adoption was to be arranged; and the baby then given to my friend. The mother worked in the show until it was obvious she was pregnant. Then, when she went into labor, I had her admitted to the obstetrical service, where she had a baby boy. When the baby was brought to the mother, it became apparent that there could be no separation, and, in spite of our well-laid plans, the adoption was off.

In due course of time, she returned to the show with the baby. The cast, including Gypsy, took up a collection to feed and support the baby and, when the mother was strong enough, she joined the troupe on the road, traveling with the baby.

I learned two things from this experience: first, whatever their intentions, most girls will not part with their babies; and, secondly, that usually little babies do not starve and are taken care of. I also learned, and have seen over the years, that theatre people are very sentimental.

CLUBS

A club is defined by Dr. Johnson to be "an assembly of good fellows meeting under conditions." As defined by another authority, it is "an association of persons subjected to particular rules."

During the years after college, living in New York, one of the first clubs I wanted to join was the Yale Club, which carried on the Yale identification I enjoyed. I don't think the Yale Club met the conditions defined by Johnson. It was composed of Yale graduates and, in addition, almost anyone who had a Yale connection. I had an uncle who had only attended Yale for one day but he was such a popular Eli that he was almost elected president of the club.

When I became a member, the club was at 44th Street and Vanderbilt Avenue, where it still stands today. There have been few changes, except that space is now shared by several other university clubs. Of course, Yale today is coeducational and there are many lovely ladies about. It is really a small hotel with fine facilities, including a library, swimming pool, squash courts and comfortable rooms, if you want to stay there. I was proud to be a member and have used it frequently all through my life.

In the early days, it had a number of traditions, which are no longer observed. The one I most loved was the special Yale train which, after a Yale-Princeton game or a Yale-Harvard game, would be met here in New York by a band and the passengers would be escorted to the Club for further refreshments. This, of course, when we won.

I also used the club to swim and to play squash. The big game

"The Racquet and Tennis Club," by William A. Moore.

was squash tennis, which is no longer played. It is a much faster and more difficult game to play than squash racquets, which is played there today.

The Racquet & Tennis Club had just moved at that time from 27 West 43rd Street to 370 Park Avenue, where it stands today. The Racquet was considered a fine club for a young man and is still. The architecture is intended to be that of a Florentine palace, although actually it is more like a fortress; the nobles of the period were frequently at war with each other! The Racquet was a place where games of all kinds could be played.

I was fairly innocent at the time of what election to that great club meant, with its long social background dating back to 1875.

There was a waiting list. In fact, sons of members were often placed on the list soon after birth in much the same way as they were entered for preparatory schools.

I was fortunate to have as a backer, my uncle, Harry Gruner, who was a popular member of the club. He had taken a fancy to me. He liked the fact that I had gone to Yale and that I played games. Uncle Harry was the prototype of a member. He was on "The Street," with a seat on the Stock Exchange, and was known as a "bear." I remember, as if to emphasize this, that he had a bear rug in his apartment.

The protocol for membership was the same then as it is today. A candidate needed a proposer, a seconder and a number of supporting letters. When you are young, as I was, and in fact, I was still in medical school, your sphere of acquaintance with members is limited. I did, of course, know the Emmet family, all of whom were members. However, Uncle Harry proceeded and, as was the custom, took me around to meet the managers of the club, to be "looked over," as it were. As most of the club managers were in Wall Street, I met him at the Stock Exchange and off we went. When you are very young, this can be somewhat of an ordeal. (I remembered that I had failed to make a Yale fraternity.) The questions asked me were what you might expect. "Where did you go to school?" St. Paul's was fine, but I had the feeling Harvard might have been better than Yale and I wasn't sure about Princeton.

The managers at that time included Alfred Hoyt, Reginald Fincke, Percy R. Pyne II, George Whitney and Charles Morgan, all of whom seemed very friendly. My uncle then announced that I was to meet the secretary of the club (1912–1936), Sherman Day, who was a lawyer. As far as Uncle Harry was concerned, no one could be elected to the club without Sherman Day's approval. He was a bachelor and the Racquet was his family. He was the most conscientious and hardworking officer in the history of the club. Although I was prepared for a difficult time, the interview with Sherman Day was not terrifying. Actually, he seemed interested that I was going into medicine.

After I left his office, my uncle went back to talk further with him. Following this, Uncle Harry took me to Eberly's, a popular spot for stockbrokers to get a drink in the afternoon. After we sat down, he said to me, "I know this has not been an easy afternoon, but Sherman Day liked you, and I think you are in." So it was and, a few days later, the notice of my election arrived in the mail, together with a bill for the dues.

My father said he would help me with the dues but I was in

for a further surprise. In those days, I always had breakfast with my father before taking off for medical school. This particular morning, I found, alongside the Racquet & Tennis bill, a check for three thousand dollars. My father said: "This is my present to you of a life membership in the Club. There may come a time in your life when it will be difficult to pay your yearly dues and I want you to always be a member of this great club."

How right he was! This was before the depression years, and often, we all know, pressures appear, and the luxury of a club membership has to be carefully considered. At that time, he did not realize that this club would play an important part in my life and that I would someday myself become a manager of the club, as I have been for the past twenty years.

Some things have changed since 1923, when I first became a member. We still have a distinctive club tie with the crossed bats on a blue or red background, but the Racquet Club hat-band, worn on the summer straw hat, is no longer, as straw hats now rarely appear in summer. Five o'clock would find the bar filled with brokers, after the close of the Stock Exchange, but no longer, as the membership is more diversified. On the other hand, court games are played at lunch time and in the evening, just as they were in the twenties.

Another change in custom is that of dressing. The Racquet has one of the finest dressing rooms in the country. At that time, dressing for dinner was a common custom and many members kept dress clothes and a few suits at the club, particularly if they lived out of town.

I remember also Johnny Davis, a club employee, who took care of all special requests of the members. He was like the porter of an English club. It was said that, if you had to go to Europe suddenly, he could get you off the same day, including a passport.

You could stay overnight at the Club, sleeping on one of the couches in the dressing room, and you paid five dollars in the morning for that privilege. No matter what condition a member was in, he could always get home for, in front of the club at all times, was a man with a horse cab to take you home.

There was another wonderful custom. If there was a big sporting event, such as a prize fight, the club would obtain a block of tickets and, after dinner at the club, members would go as a group.

My early club life at the R&T was great fun. Even though I was a medical student, I found time to play games and most of the time was on the third floor where the courts began. As I have often said, games are where you make friends who remain friends throughout the rest of your life.

The Racquet Club was known to have great professionals in all of its court games and they were an important part of a player's life. Some years later, I met Eddie Rogers who was, in my opinion, one of the great professionals. He ended my squash racquets career for the superior game of racquets and I rarely played squash after that.

The club at that period had the reputation that most of its membership were rich, drank heavily and led non-productive lives. I felt this to be unfair. Today, as a manager, I see many of the candidates for membership, and they are from all professions and appear headed for distinguished careers.

There are two customs which are supposed to be observed. One is that a lady's name is never to be mentioned in the bar room, and the other, that when one enters the club, business is to be left behind. There was a rule in the early days, in fact, that no briefcase could be brought above the first floor.

My father belonged to a small club, the Calumet Club, where he often went for lunch. It no longer exists. He also enjoyed the New York Athletic Club, where he often took me, particularly during the time when I was fencing.

Early in my life, my father introduced me to Masonry, which he loved. He liked the whole Masonic idea of fraternity, belief in God, ritual. At an early age, he introduced me to his lodge. In 1923, I became a Master Mason, and he was very pleased.

My father had been very interested in Rotary. He was a bashful man and he found Rotary clubs a very useful way to meet people. In Rotary, you call people by their first name; that is part of the Rotary tradition. Rotarians have a sort of comraderie which my father was not quite used to but which he found quite enjoyable all his life. Later on, I joined as well. Father was not a talkative man and was quite different from the usual outgoing Rotarian, but he made many friends.

He impressed me with the importance of getting to know people. This is essential for a doctor in practice, where there are many different levels of patients, all from different backgrounds.

GAMES I HAVE PLAYED

What are the benefits from playing games? I can recall when my highest ambition in life was to secure a place on my school team and to win a "letter." It was very important to me to wear a sweater representing my school, telling the world that I was an athlete of distinction. It was equally important that I made friends in doing this, some of whom have remained friends during all my lifetime, but, at the time, I did not know this. Later,

I played only for exercise and, if I won or lost, only I was concerned. I then became aware of other benefits from playing games, perhaps more of a psychiatric nature. Everyone has periods of anxiety in his life and I was grateful for a game like squash or racquets which compelled me, for an hour or two, and, in the case of golf, for an even longer time, to withdraw from everything else, to concentrate on the game. I am frank to say that I always liked to win, but whether I won or lost, the main thing is that it is hard to think of anything else when you are on a racquet court watching a fast-moving ball or on a golf course putting green, faced with the always miserable three-footer. There is no doubt that sport contributes not only to physical wellbeing, but also to mental health, which is an indispensable part of the good life.

In New York in the twenties, there were four court games played or perhaps five, if you include handball. These were squash, racquets, tennis (court tennis or real tennis, as it is called) and squash tennis. Squash racquets and squash tennis were played in the college clubs and in some of the larger clubs, such as the University Club and the New York Athletic Club, but racquets and court tennis were played only at the Racquet & Tennis Club, which had the only courts in the city. As a result, these two games were played by only comparatively few people and, for a number of reasons, still are. In fact, the average person, who has not seen these games played, does not even have the faintest idea what they are all about. A description is very difficult and the general public is not interested, although the recent surge of attention to squash racquets has led to public courts and a greater number of players. Today, like soccer, squash racquets enjoys the popularity and interest which it surely deserves.

I liked playing squash racquets and my school training found me good enough to play in the interclub matches and the local tournaments. The Yale Club was my home base and the first place that I played in New York. But the Racquet & Tennis Club is the finest club in the world for court games. Not only were courts available but, for the first time, it was possible for me to play with professionals. Unless one has played games, it is impossible to realize how important a role the professional plays. Not only does he teach the game and is always available to play, but he encourages the players, arranges games and, in addition, often becomes a close friend. This was true at the Racquet Club, where Eddie Rogers, the head professional, became my good friend and remained so all my life.

I played a lot of squash racquets for several years, with varying success. I came near to winning the Racquet & Tennis Club championship and did manage to win the Yale Club championship in 1931. Probably this was my greatest triumph in this game. I made many close friends playing at the various clubs and in tournaments. I have said many times that one makes good friends playing games.

Although I am now convinced of the importance of physical fitness in young men, I did not think about it at that time and did not train, as perhaps one should when one is playing top competitive squash. I do remember coming home after an all-out game, exhausted and with a complete loss of appetite, but outside of that, this kind of exercise, in my opinion, can do you nothing but good. I kept on playing squash, but something happened that turned my interest and attention to what I think is the greatest court game, racquets.

Eddie Rogers took me one day into the racquet court. There were two at the Racquet & Tennis Club. He handed me a racquet, told me the proper way to hold it and asked me to hit a racquet ball to the front wall. That did it because, from that point on, I never went back to squash racquets, which I had played so much.

I didn't know then what the Marquis of Salisbury, speaking about racquets in England, had said: "It is one of the most historic games still played in this country. In the past one hundred years many thousands of young men have learnt to play racquets at the public schools. They have acquired speed of eye, swiftness of foot and strength of arm. They have come to appreciate the meaning of good sportsmanship and the demands of unselfish partnership, and they have enjoyed a magnificent game." I was to learn all this during the coming years. The feeling of hitting a racquet ball is like that of no other court game and is impossible to describe, as is the sound one hears as the ball comes audibly in contact with the wall. This sound and sensation can even be imparted to the gallery. I made up my mind that I would learn this game, regardless of its difficulty.

I soon found out a lot of things I didn't know and Eddie Rogers had not told me when I began to take lessons from him. Although the appearance and implements are similar between the two games, squash racquets and racquets, as games they have little in common. There are many differences in the two games. Speed has been said to be the chief attraction of racquets, not speed for the sake of speed, but for the control that a man shows over it.

I soon found out that this game was played by very few and that there were less than a dozen courts in the United States and Canada. The reasons for this were obvious. The cost of building a court, which is made of slate, was astronomical. No new courts had been built in many years when I started to play. The cost of playing was another consideration; the game was played by a wealthy minority. There were very few players, although it seemed to me they were all good. I determined to learn the game and really worked at it.

The Racquet Club had, besides Eddie Rogers, several other professionals who had been imported from England; I had the opportunity of playing with all of them.

There are a number of discouraging features of the game that could cause a new player to give up in a hurry. The return of service is exceedingly difficult and anyone with a good service, at the time I began to play, could prevent me from ever or only occasionally returning the ball at all. It was very like what we see in tennis today—a continuous series of aces, where an opponent does not even touch the ball. To learn to return a good service takes hours of practice. On the other side of the coin, to learn to serve well takes an equal amount of time. As far as stroke is concerned, most of the good players had learned the game in some place like Tuxedo, where there had been a court since the turn of the century.

The difficulty of playing racquets makes it essential to be taught by a professional and Eddie Rogers was one of the all-time greats. I remember how he taught me to hold the racquet with the proper grip. He threw his racquet on the floor and then told me to pick it up. There is only one way to do this and that is the proper way to hold it.

He also had a method for teaching the beginner to hit the ball to the front wall. He would stand opposite you and, with a basket of balls, bounce the ball off the back wall, so that it would be directly in front of you. You then would hit the ball to the front wall. In actual play, the ball often does just this, so it is a particularly useful way to learn the proper stroke.

Service can only be learned by long practice, so that the proper length can be obtained and the ball does not come off the back wall, giving your opponent an easy return. Rogers would make me stay in the service box until I was exhausted, serving to him both in the right and left hand courts. There were very few days that I did not get a lesson from him and, if I did not, I practiced by myself which, as in golf, you can do.

After a time, I was ready to play against players like myself,

The great "Pro," Pierre Etchebaster.

who had just begun. As for playing with the few good players at that time, it would have been difficult to get even a few points per game.

When I started, there were two players who completely dominated the game in this country and it seemed unlikely anyone had a chance against them. Clarence Pell had won the racquet singles championship of America from 1915 to 1928, with three exceptions, when S. G. Mortimer beat him, and, playing as a

To Dr. Bishop, in Souvenir of our good time in the court and hoping, reading those lignes you will enjoy more our beautiful game of "Court Tennis"

with my best wishes

Pierre Etchebaster

"Pierre's Book" Inscription.

doubles team, except on a few occasions, they were the American champions during those years.

Racquets was a game I loved and this game exposed me to the most ancient of court games, which is called court tennis in this country, tennis or real tennis or royal tennis in England and *jeu de paume* in France. There were only seven courts in this country and the only people who understood the game at all were those who played it. The American champion, when I first saw or heard about the game was Jay Gould, who had a long career as champion from 1906–1925. He completely dominated the game, very much like Clarence Pell did in racquets.

I tried to learn the game, but was so occupied with racquets that it wasn't until the middle thirties that I felt I had any real understanding of it. At that time, Pierre Etchebaster had come to the club as a professional. He was the greatest player and teacher of all time. Pierre inspired everyone who played with him. He took as much trouble with every pupil who took lessons from him as if he were about to produce a new champion.

The tennis court itself is extremely complicated and I honestly believe that it cannot be described without one actually seeing it. Comparing it with other court games, you note many peculiarities, the most interesting being that in no other court game can you, under certain circumstances, deliberately not return the ball to your opponent, but have the option of making a better shot at a later time. In no other court game is the scoring so complicated that a professional has to be employed to keep track of the score.

Although there is a great difference between tennis and racquets, both in stroke and court, there has always been a close connection between the two games. Most racquet players like myself, have played some tennis. The great English player, E. W. Baerlein, speaks rather poetically about the difficulty of learning tennis (and the same might be said about racquets): "Tennis is a difficult and ingenious mistress, holding out promises never to be fulfilled, of favors for those who pursue her in an unworthy manner. Let the young suitor beware of the appearance of early success, gained by length and placing, for it is not by these means that the Queen (perhaps it should be the King, but no matter) of games can be won. There is no short-cut to her heart. She will yield to none who have not shown their proper worth by a proper apprenticeship to the correct stroke."

In my opinion, racquets is the king of games and tennis the queen.

H. A. Harris states in *Sport in Britain: Its Origins and Development*: "There is no realm of human activity about which it is more difficult to think clearly than sport. From one point of view it is useless and aimless. It is the antithesis to a man's work in life by which he serves the community and earns his living and it is precisely because it is the opposite of that purposeful business that it affords an incomparable medium of refreshment and recreation in leisure hours."

Chapter XI

RELIGION

My mother and father were members of St. Thomas Episcopal Church on Fifth Avenue and 53rd Street. I learned that my father had been brought up in what was called the Dutch Reformed Church. My father's brother, Ellis, was a minister. My mother's family, on her father's side, were Lutherans. As a child, I would often attend services at St. Patrick's with my nanny, who was a Roman Catholic.

My father had attended St. Paul's School, as I did later on, and we both came under the Episcopalian "roof." George Shattuck, Episcopal clergyman and founder of the school believed that: "Boys must be educated both in spirituality and nature, for the things of this world are engrossing, but boys ought to be trained not only for this life, but so as to enter into and enjoy unseen realities. The life of this world is short and uncertain."

My father numbered among his friends a number of members of the ministry, including his college roommate, Evartson Cobb, a prominent New York minister in later life.

As I was first sent to St. Bernard's School, where both headmasters were of the Church of England, and later to St. Paul's School, it is not surprising that I ended up an Episcopalian.

At St. Paul's, we attended chapel every morning and twice on Sunday. Many boys later told me that, after leaving St. Paul's, they avoided churchgoing. I was one of those and went little during my college years, except for Christmas and Easter. At Yale, I became aware of other faiths besides my own and recognized the importance of interfaith, understanding which would play an important part in my life as a physician.

While at medical school, I again took a more active role in the church and, for a time, I taught Sunday School. I don't think I was very good at it, but it gave me the opportunity to re-study the Bible stories, which have always interested children as well as adults. I never did find out what happened to Daniel in the lion's den, and the story of Jonah and the whale was also difficult to explain. In a recent sermon by a born-again Christian, it was explained that Daniel's character kept him alive and that the lion would not eat such a good man.

At medical school, I also met young men of the Jewish faith, and I learned of the importance of their religious holidays, which were observed, it seemed to me, in a very dedicated manner. I could not imagine fasting for a whole day, as is done on the Day of Atonement.

I would be exposed to other great religions in later life, but this was the beginning of my realization that there were other faiths beside Christianity.

My father frequently talked to me about the relationship between medicine and religion, and these are his words: "I must include in my conception of medicine the whole art and science of healing and by religion I must ask you to understand that fundamental attribute of human nature that needs expression in many churches and many creeds. When it comes to the question of healing, the clergyman and the doctor must march hand in hand in bringing to the relief of human suffering the broad science of therapeutics and the fundamental knowledge of the needs of the spirit. Neither religion nor science is meant to ignore the other, and in the light of modern knowledge we are coming to the understanding that what is deepest and most fundamental in religion is reinforced and not belittled by science."

In modern times, Norman Vincent Peale has emphasized this approach.

Coming under the influence of these beliefs, I understood the importance of religion to the practicing physician and that an awareness of other faiths than my own might help me better care for my patients as well as enrich my own life.

Chapter XII

MARRIAGE

W<small>HEN</small> I <small>WAS A</small> F<small>OURTH</small> Y<small>EAR</small> <small>MEDICAL STUDENT</small>, I often went to East Hampton during the summer for vacations. I usually stayed at the Hunting Inn.

There were a number of Saturday night parties, where young men were in demand. At that time I had a great friend, Jack Draper, and we frequently went to these parties together. Jack was a member of the famous artistic Draper family.

At one of these parties, I met Kathleen Sinclair, whose family was living at East Hampton at that time. Later on, I was told that she had picked me because Jack Draper was quite tall and I was nearer her own size. Like other young men, still at school, and not yet established in careers, Jack and I were interested in having a good time, and not ready for permanent attachments but, as it turned out, this was not the case as far as I was concerned, because, after I met Kitty, we both fell in love and later became engaged.

We were married on June 17, 1925 at St. Thomas Church on Fifth Avenue. After the ceremony, we traveled by train to California and then by ship to Honolulu.

On board ship, I nearly became a casualty. There was a game played by two people, where a cracker was placed on top of each person's head; each person was blindfolded and handed a rolled-up newspaper. Then, sitting, facing each other, the object of the game was to break the cracker on your opponent's head. In my case, my opponent was an Irish priest from Fordham University, who had probably played football for the school, and he nearly put me away with a blow on the head, which was very unsettling for my bride.

When we got to Honolulu, I became interested in going to Molokai, where there was a leper colony. I was told that if I went there, she would leave me forever. Needless to say, I immediately gave up Molokai.

When we returned to New York, I spent that fall in my father's office, before beginning my internship at Bellevue in January.

June 17, 1925. Ingersoll, Bride and Groom, Julia Morley.

Chapter XIII

EPILOGUE

THIS HAS BEEN THE STORY of growing up in New York as a privileged individual, who received the best education available and who finally graduated from medical school.

After my internship at Bellevue, I went into my father's office as his assistant, although I tried to develop a practice of my own. My father was, at that time, one of the best-known heart specialists in the world and had a large practice, which he hoped to eventually turn over to me. My knowledge of heart disease was what I learned at Bellevue and I could not honestly call myself a "specialist." I did learn what I could from my father and took what few post-graduate courses were available in New York.

As his assistant, I got to know many of his patients, as I was required to take the history and to do a physical examination on each one. I was also exposed to the limited technology available at that time, as my father had instruments not routinely in use in the offices of other doctors. In this day and age, these instruments would be considered primitive.

I enjoyed my association with my father. I was paid a salary and did not have any responsibility for the overhead of the office, nor did I have direct responsibility for the medical management of patients.

Every day I spent with my father, I felt that I learned something important.

A year went by and, one morning, my father announced that he and my mother were going on a cruise around the world and would be away four months. I was to "carry on" the practice.

A very difficult period followed, which I might say did little good to my self-image. Many patients, on hearing that my father was away, postponed their visits until his return. A few agreed to see the young doctor because their histories were in the office. These came, with the understanding that they would, of course, see my father on his return. New patients postponed coming. Gradually, the practice diminished.

When my father and mother returned, another surprise awaited. He announced that he was retiring, although he would be available for consultation.

I have often wondered whether that trip was his way of bowing out and thrusting me "onstage."

I was now on my own. I continued the practice of cardiology for the next fifty years.